新编剑桥商务英语应试辅导用书

丛书主编　周之南
分册主编　李慧杰
副 主 编　陈　楠　秦　怡

BEC 写作全攻略 中级

SUCCESS WITH BEC VANTAGE

中国财经出版传媒集团
经济科学出版社
Economic Science Press

图书在版编目（CIP）数据

BEC写作全攻略：中级/周之南主编；李慧杰分册主编．
—北京：经济科学出版社，2018.6（2019.6重印）
ISBN 978－7－5141－9271－1

Ⅰ.①B…　Ⅱ.①周…②李…　Ⅲ.①商务－英语－写作－自学参考资料　Ⅳ.①F7

中国版本图书馆CIP数据核字（2018）第090656号

责任编辑：孙怡虹　刘　博
责任校对：徐领柱
版式设计：齐　杰
责任印制：王世伟

BEC写作全攻略（中级）
丛书主编　周之南
分册主编　李慧杰
经济科学出版社出版、发行　新华书店经销
社址：北京市海淀区阜成路甲28号　邮编：100142
总编部电话：010－88191217　发行部电话：010－88191522
网址：www.esp.com.cn
电子邮件：esp@esp.com.cn
天猫网店：经济科学出版社旗舰店
网址：http://jjkxcbs.tmall.com
北京密兴印刷有限公司印装
710×1000　16开　13.75印张　275000字
2018年11月第1版　2019年6月第2次印刷
ISBN 978－7－5141－9271－1　定价：36.00元
（图书出现印装问题，本社负责调换。电话：010－88191510）

主编及主要编者简介

李慧杰：女，哈尔滨工业大学外国语学院教授，上海外国语大学英语语言文学博士学位。具有20多年英语教学经验，获多项省部级教学和科研成果奖。BEC口语考试考官。

陈楠：女，哈尔滨工业大学外国语学院教师，双硕士学位：哈尔滨工业大学应用语言学硕士学位，新加坡南洋理工应用语言学硕士学位。具有10多年英语教学经验，多次获得省级和校级教学比赛奖项。BEC口语考试考官。

秦怡：女，哈尔滨工业大学外国语学院副教授，哈尔滨工业大学应用语言学硕士学位。具有20多年英语教学经验。

路遥：女，黑龙江中医药大学公共外语教研部教师，黑龙江大学英语语言文学硕士学位，天津师范大学比较文学与世界文学专业博士。具有10余年英语教学经验，多次获得省级和校级教学比赛奖项。

周洁：女，哈尔滨工业大学外国语学院教师，哈尔滨工业大学应用语言学硕士学位。具有近20年英语教学经验。BEC口语考试考官。

前　言 Preface

众所周知，随着世界经济全球化步伐日益加快，中国经济与世界经济逐步接轨，国际商务往来日益频繁。语言作为一种必不可少的沟通桥梁，正在逐渐发挥它不可替代的重要作用。商务英语是一种在工作环境中使用的、世界通用的语言，适用于政府机关、事业单位、企业、商社等各种机构的日常公务和商贸活动。

商务英语证书（BEC）是教育部考试中心和英国剑桥大学考试委员会合作，根据公务或商务工作的实际需要，对考生在一般工作环境下和商务活动中使用英语的能力从听、说、读、写四个方面进行全面考查，对成绩合格者提供由英国剑桥大学考试委员会颁发的标准统一的成绩证书。由于其颁发机构的权威性，该证书在一百多个国家和地区的商业企业部门获得认可，成为证明证书持有者英语能力的首选，也是在所有举办该项考试的国家和地区求职的“通行证”。

《BEC 写作全攻略》（初、中、高级）系列丛书则是专门为备考剑桥商务英语证书（Business English Certificate）而量身编写的配套用书。它有效地解决了国内考生在备考商务英语初、中、高级系列考试时，由于教材为国外原版引进，文化背景不同而导致的考生理解力有限的问题；同时它也满足了广大考生对写作进行专项辅导的要求，使商务英语的学习更加具体，解决了课堂教学兼顾听、说、读、写而导致的大而不精的问题。基于这些优势，本丛书重点体现了以下几个特点：

1. 分类详解，涵盖面广

BEC 考试分为初、中、高三个级别的考试。在每个级别的考试中，写作部分都包括两个任务：PART ONE 和 PART TWO。在同一级别的考试中，两个任务对写作的篇幅、类型和语言考察的侧重点都有明显不同的要求；在不同级别之间，相同的写作任务要求考生完成的写作篇幅、类型和文体也不相同。比如，在 BEC 初级的 PART ONE 中，考生应当完成一个简短的便条、留言条、备忘录或者电子邮件的写作；而在 BEC 高级的 PART ONE 中，考生则应依据图表写一个商务报告。因此，本丛书的每一册都分别详细地介绍了写作任务 1 和写作任务 2。并且在每个任务当中，又一一讲解了各种体裁的写作特点。

2. 立足真题，接近考试

由于是关于写作的针对性极强的书籍，因此在本丛书中必不可少地要出现大量写作练习题和写作范文。BEC 考试不同于其他国内英语语言类考试，它的写作会给考生模拟一个写作环境，比如简短的写作背景描述、图表、假定考生的作者身份或者写作角度等。因此，在本丛书中出现的写作题目要求大部分均来自历年的考试真题，或者由丛书作者依据剑桥大学考试委员会提供的考试手册要求，精心挑选国外商务或公务第一手素材编写而成。这样就使整套丛书更加接近 BEC 考试的真实环境和难度，使考生在最初备考时，就已经站在了和 BEC 相近的水平线上。有了明确的标准，才能保证最佳的学习质量。

3. 范文充足，讲解细致

本套丛书中出现的每个写作范例或练习，均配有相应的范文。这些范文大都是作者在教学第一线积累的学生作文，或者由作者亲自撰写，因此能鲜明地体现广大考生在写作当中出现的普遍性的问题，具有极强的代表性；由作者撰写的范文也均依据剑桥大学考试委员会提供的写作要求，具有鲜明的示范性。

此外，对于一些典型的范文，本丛书也做了细致的讲解。从词汇到篇章，从搭配到逻辑，从结构到思想，从体裁到文体，均做出了详细的说明。这也解决了许多年以来，广大考生没有系统地学习过英文篇章的撰写，写作时无从下手、考虑不周、表达不到位等诸多问题。

4. 应用性强，学以致用

国内学生多年的英语写作大都侧重于语法、词汇等语言层面上的学习，他们很少能将语言应用于真正意义上的工作或商务活动。更不要谈及用英语来创作正式、非正式的信函、撰写工作年度报告，商务分析、商务策划、工作备忘录等一系列非常具体的商务文章。因此，在校大中专生尽管学习了多年英语，但是一旦走上工作岗位，他们就会发觉自己学习的知识和实际工作之间有一定的距离。本丛书十分及时地解决了这个问题。丛书中提供了大量的商务和公务环境，并且配有充足的范例和讲解，这样一来，广大学生可以提前进行工作演练，为今后的实践应用积累足够的知识和经验，真正做到学以致用。

由于编者水平有限，编写时间仓促，不当和错误之处在所难免，欢迎广大读者批评指正。

编者
2018 年 5 月

目 录 Contents

Week 1

明确任务：了解要求+确定目标

Day 1

了解 BEC 中级写作考试

1. BEC 等级证书和剑桥英语分数量表以及雅思成绩的对应

商务英语证书考试（BEC）是英国剑桥考试委员会开发的系列英语考试中的一种。BEC 已经被超过 100 万证书持有者用来证明其具备职场所必需的英语技能。BEC 考试分初级（Preliminary）、中级（Vantage）和高级（Higher）三个等级。BEC 证书与语言能力国际公认标准——欧洲语言共同参考框架（CEFR）相对应。

	级　别	剑桥英语分数量表	IELTS 雅思成绩
CEFR C1	BEC Higher 高级	200 ~ 204	8
		191 ~ 199	7. 5
		185 ~ 190	7
CEFR B2	BEC Vantage 中级	176 ~ 184	6. 5
		169 ~ 175	6
		162 ~ 168	5. 5
CEFR B1	BEC Preliminary 初级	154 ~ 161	5
		147 ~ 153	4. 5
		142 ~ 146	4

在中国，BEC 考试由中英双方合办。英国剑桥大学考试委员会负责命题、阅卷和颁发证书。中国教育部考试中心负责报名、印制试卷和组织考试。BEC 中级考试包括听力、阅读、写作和口语四个组成部分，各占总成绩的 1/4，其中写作部分与听、说、读相比，因其考查形式固定，内容要求有限，因而最易通过自学和练习而得到较为理想的成绩。

2. BEC 中级写作任务构成

BEC 中级写作要求考生完成两项任务：一项是进行公司内部的事务沟通，如同事间使用电子邮件、备忘录、便条等形式传递信息；另一项是从整个公司或部门的角度，写一封商务信函与其他公司沟通，或针对某一项业务，写一份商务报告，或写一份建议书。

试卷形式	试卷由两个商务写作任务构成，答题时需考虑提供的场景、写作的目的和目标读者
答题时间	45 分钟
组成部分	两部分组成，PART ONE 和 PART TWO
任务数量	2 个（均为必答题）
任务类型	任务 1 要求写一篇用于公司内部交流的短文； 任务 2 要求写一封商务信函，或一份商务报告，或一份建议书
答题方式	考生在答题册上作答
分值	第一部分占写作总分的 1/3，第二部分占写作总分的 2/3

➢任务 1

任务类型	内部商务往来 internal business correspondence
出题形式	用文字说明考题情景和答题要点 （如果任务形式是便条或电子邮件，则答题格式事先给出）
答题形式	• 便函 message • 备忘录 memo • 电子邮件 email • 便条 note （指定用其中一种形式答题）

续表

写作目的	• 告知信息 • 布置安排 • 征求意见 • 询问信息 • 求助申请 • 推荐建议等
语言风格	中性/非正式
字数要求	40 ~ 50 词

➢任务 2

任务类型	• 商务往来信函 business correspondence • 商务报告 short report • 建议书 proposal （以其中一种形式出题）
出题形式	题目中除用文字说明考题情景外，还可能有来自商务往来中的信函、传真或电子邮件；或来自公司内部的便条、备忘录或电子邮件；或来自相关通知、广告、图表等。要点通常以手写标注的形式给出 （如果任务形式是传真或电子邮件，则答题格式事先给出）
答题形式	• 信函 letter • 传真 fax • 电子邮件 email • 备忘录 memo • 报告 report • 建议书 proposal （指定用其中一种形式答题）

续表

写作目的	商务信函 • 订购、询问 • 投诉、道歉 • 解释、说明 • 告知变化 • 确认信息 • 邀请等 商务报告 • 描述说明 • 分析归纳 建议书 • 提供信息 • 分析归纳 • 提出建议 • 说服接受等
语言风格	中性/正式
字数要求	120～140 词

Day 2

解析 BEC 中级写作的任务与要求

1. 任务 1 解析

➢任务 1 解析

任务 1 考查考生能够在公司内部通过英语写作进行事务沟通的能力。

任务 1 题目的文字说明（指导语）包含以下内容：

- 情景的简要描述及写作人和目标阅读人的相关信息
- 任务形式，如备忘录、便条等
- 答题的内容点

➢任务 1 答题步骤

- 仔细阅读答题要求和答题要点
- 写初稿，句子要简洁明了
- 检查初稿，确保包含所有要点信息
- 核查字数，合理删除不必要单词
- 誊写初稿到答题纸，字迹清晰工整

➢任务1　举例

PART ONE

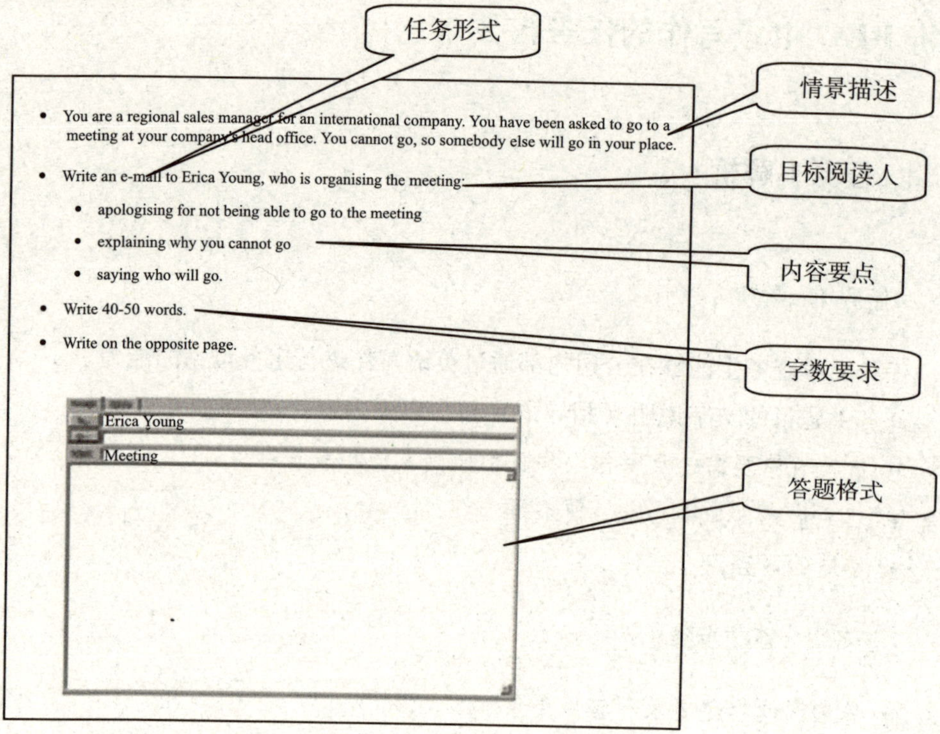

考生需要做到以下几点：

- 根据情景写一篇用于公司内部交流的短文
- 知道如何简洁地使用商务语言
- 短文的长度在40～50词之内
- 包括所有3个内容要点
- 提供明了切题的事实性信息，避免不必要的解释
- 如果要求写备忘录或电子邮件，不需考虑收发人、日期、主题等细节，直接写正文

2. 任务2解析

➢任务2 解析

任务2题目中的文字说明包括以下内容：

- 写作情景的说明
- 需要完成的任务
- 目标阅读人

任务2的题目中还可能包括：

- 一段或几段文字，置于便条、信函、传真、广告或图表等形式之中
- 需要谈及的内容点，通常是手写标注的形式

任务2的写作形式如果是电子邮件或传真，则格式会事先给出。

任务2只考察下列三种形式之一，是必答题。

- 商务往来信函
- 商务报告
- 商务建议书

➢任务2 答题步骤

- 仔细阅读答题要求
- 阅读所有给定材料，包括图表、备忘录等
- 在给定材料中标示出所有要包括在作文中的要点
- 先写初稿，确保包括所有要点
- 检查作文长度，如果过短，查看是否遗漏重要信息；如果过长，改写某些句子，减少字数
- 誊写初稿到答题纸，字迹清晰工整

➢任务 2　举例

PART TWO

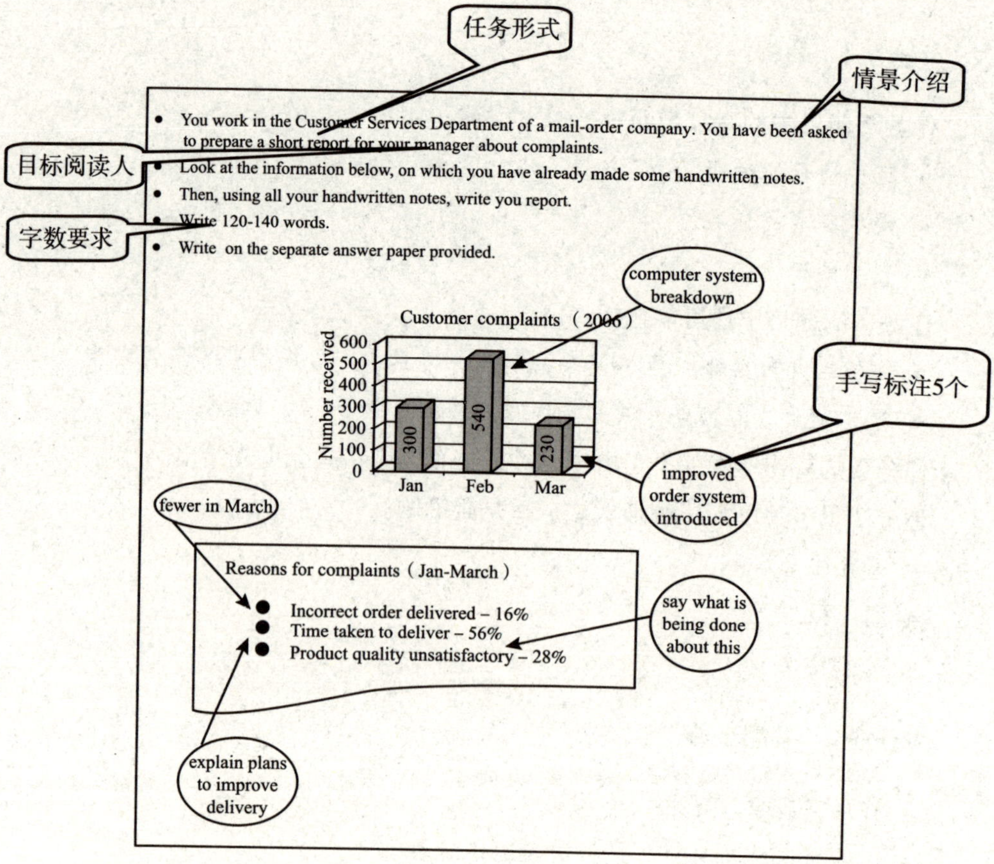

考生需要做到以下几点：

- 切题
- 给出目标阅读人需要的所有信息
- 必要时加入自己的信息
- 确保事实性信息清晰、切题

考生答题应该考虑所写的文章对目标阅读人会产生什么样的影响：

- 文章是否友好礼貌？
- 行文是否适合阅读人的身份？

考生应该表现出熟练掌握丰富的词汇和语法结构：

- 对关键词能够变换使用
- 对题目中给出的句子能够换词表达
- 文中使用富于变化的语法结构

考生对答题格式应该知道如下几点：

- 建议书和报告的格式没有显著区别
- 报告的结构必须清晰
- 报告中不应包含信件的特征
- 信件中应包含开头和结尾格式
- 信件中不需邮寄地址
- 传真中不需写明具体标题（fax header）
- 备忘录中不需包括发件人、收件人、日期、主题等信息
- 电子邮件中不需包括发件人、收件人、日期、主题等信息

Day 3

知晓 BEC 中级写作常见话题

BEC 中级考试手册中所提及的考试的所有组成部分，都出自以下 10 个话题领域（topic area）：

（1）身份介绍（personal identification）
（2）工作环境与日常事务（the office，general business，environment and routine）
（3）接待与闲暇活动（entertainment of clients，free time，relationships with colleagues and clients）
（4）商务旅行与会议（travels and meetings）
（5）记录电话信息（using the telephone）
（6）健康与安全（health and safety）
（7）购买与销售（buying and selling）
（8）公司结构、系统及程序（company structure，systems and processes）
（9）产品与服务（products and services）
（10）成果与成就（results and achievements）

然而，BEC 中级写作更多地、较具体地涉及以下商务活动：

➢人力资源（human resources）

- 员工培训 staff development and training
- 工作描述 job description
- 工作满意度 job satisfaction
- 询问信 enquiry letter
- 申请信 application letter
- 电话技巧 telephone skills

➢市场开拓（marketing）

• 促销活动	promotional activities
• 创建新品牌	branding
• 新产品开发	new product development
• 展销会展位	a stand at a trade fair
• 建立合作关系	establishing relationship
• 谈判	negotiating

➢开展新业务（starting new business activities）

• 初始资金投入	financing the start-up
• 进入新城市	starting up in a new location
• 寻找办公场所	looking for a new office
• 表达工作思路	presenting new ideas
• 举办销售会议	holding a sales conference

➢商务旅行（business travels）

• 宾馆和机票	hotels and flight tickets
• 准备商务会议	preparing for business conferences
• 会议报销	covering business expenses
• 谈论/汇报商务会议	talking/reporting a business meeting

➢新技术、创新和变动（new technologies，innovation and changes）

• 引进新技术	introducing new technologies
• 工作中的变动	changes in work
• 公司网页设计/更新	designing/updating company websites
• 制定新规章制度	laying down new rules/regulations
• 业务外包	outsourcing
• 建立分厂	off shoring

➤与客户沟通（customer relationship management）

• 客户满意度	customer satisfaction
• 客户忠诚度	customer loyalty
• 处理投诉	dealing with complaints
• 如何与客户沟通的培训	training in customer communication skills
• 客户沟通讨论会	seminars

Day 4

研读 BEC 中级写作评分标准

BEC 写作考试采用网上评分的方式，系统随机给评分员分配考生的作文。评分员们严格按照评分标准给出成绩。从评分标准中可以看出，目前 BEC 中级写作主要考察四个方面：**文章内容（Content）、交际效果（Communicative Achievement）、篇章组织（Organisation）和语言应用（Language）**。

文章内容项考查考生是否很好地完成所要求的任务；交际效果一项考查考生是否使用恰当的语言风格完成任务；篇章组织这一项考查考生的作文是否符合逻辑有条理；语言应用项考查考生的词汇和语法使用的丰富性和准确性。

评分员针对每一个考查项在 0 ~ 5 分范围内给出分数。

级别	文章内容	交际效果	篇章组织	语言应用
5	所有内容均与任务密切相关； 目标读者获得全部信息	能够有效地使用惯例做法完成交际任务，引起目标读者的注意，恰当地传递简单的和复杂的想法	篇章结构清晰连贯，能够使用丰富的关联手段和结构模式，整体效果良好	能够使用丰富词汇，较少使用普通词汇，用词恰当； 能够使用从简单到复杂的语法形式，用法得当灵活； 偶尔有错，但不影响交际
4	学生的表现介于 3 分和 5 分之间			
3	有少许不相关内容或少许信息遗漏； 整体来说目标读者获得了信息	能够使用惯例做法完成交际任务，引起目标读者的注意，恰当地传递简单的想法	篇章结构整体上清晰连贯，能够使用丰富的连接词和关联手段	能够恰当使用丰富的日常词汇，某些不常用词汇的使用可能出错； 能够使用从简单到比较复杂的语法形式，用法得当； 有错，但不影响交际

续表

级别	文章内容	交际效果	篇章组织	语言应用
2	学生的表现介于 1 分和 3 分之间			
1	有不相关内容，或对任务有错误的解释； 目标读者获得较少信息	整体上能够使用惯例做法完成交际任务，传递简单的想法	篇章有一定关联性，能够使用基本的连接词和少量的关联手段	能够恰当使用日常词汇，可能过度使用某些词汇； 能够使用简单的语法形式，用法得当； 有明显错误，但不影响交际
0	内容完全与任务无关； 目标读者没有获得信息	表现低于 1 分		

Day 5

分析 BEC 中级写作样文、分值及评语

PART ONE

- You are a regional sales manager of an international company. You have been asked to go to a meeting at your company' s head office. You cannot go, so somebody else will go in your place.
- Write an e-mall to Erica Young, who is organising the meeting:
    - apologising for not being able to go to the meeting
    - explaining why you cannot go
    - saying who will go
- Write 40-50 words.
- Write on the opposite page.

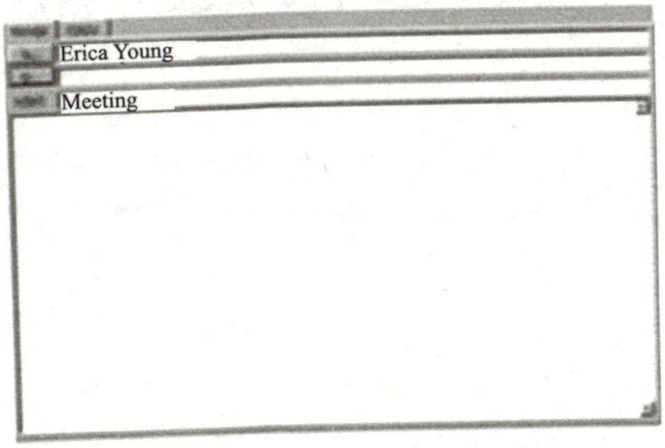

Candidate A

I'm really sorry but I'm not able to go to the meeting at our company's head office. I can't attend because of previous arrangements which I can't change.

Mr. Jan Korwalski, a very good worker, will go instead of me.

Please accept my apologies.

Marta Stefanska

Examiner comments

Subscale	*Mark*	*Examiner comments*
Content	5	All the content points are addressed and expanded where relevant to the task. The target reader would be fully informed and able to act on the information given.
Communicative Achievement	5	The conventions of the communicative task have been used effectively to hold the reader's attention, to communicate the information concisely and in an appropriate register (*I'm really sorry but*; *Please accept my apologies*).
Organisation	5	The text is well organised and coherent, using a variety of cohesive devices to good effect (*but*; *because of*; *which*).
Language	5	The range of vocabulary and grammatical forms is fully appropriate to the task and used with control and accuracy (*because of previous arrangements which I can't change*; *Jan Korwalski, a very good worker, will go instead of me*).

Candidate B

To: Erica Young

Subject: Meeting

Dear Mr Young,

Thanks for your last letter! I'm very glad to be inviated to attend the meeting at your company's head office. But first of all, I'm apologising for not being able to go to the meeting. This is due to a error of my agenda, in fact. I have a international conference that day.

I feel sorry for my absence. I'd like to recommend my personal assistant to go instead of me. His name is Jim Green. I hope this will not cause you some trouble.

Best wish yours

Chan Bo Fun

Examiner comments

Subscale	*Mark*	*Examiner comments*
Content	3	Although minor irrelevances are present (*Thanks for your last letter!*), the target reader, on the whole, would be informed.
Communicative Achievement	3	Uses the conventions of the task to hold the target reader's attention and convey the message, although the text lacks concision, which may have an adverse effect on the target reader.
Organization	3	The text is generally well organised and the ideas are linked. There is some suitable use of cohesive devices and other organisational features (*This is due to*; *that day*; *His name is*; *I hope this will not cause*), although sentences tend to be short and linking words are not always appropriately used.
Language	3	Uses a range of everyday vocabulary appropriately (*head office*; *international conference*; *absence*; *personal assistant*). There is a range of simple and complex grammatical forms. Errors are present (*inviated*; *a error*; *I feel sorry for my absence*; *Best wish yours*) but they do not impede communication.

Candidate C

To: Erica Young

C. C:

Subject: Meeting

Date: 1 June 2006

Dear ERICA!

Please! give me apologise, but I do not being able to go to the meeting. Becose I have got verry important meeting with our cluent. My colleg Andrei Ivanov go to the head office. Please fixed all our problem with him. His verry rellable person.

Examiner comments

Subscale	*Mark*	*Examiner comments*
Content	2	An attempt is made to communicate the message, but there are some irrelevances (*Please fixed all our problem with him*; *His verry rellable person*). The target reader is only partially informed since inference is required to understand which meeting is being referred to and that Andrei Ivanov will be deputising for the writer.
Communicative Achievement	1	The conventions of the task are attempted and the writer conveys straightforward ideas, but not always successfully (*I do not being able to go to the meeting*).
Organization	1	The text is mostly coherent and simple organizational features are present (*but*; *with him*) but linking words are not always appropriately used (*Becose I have got verry important meeting*).
Language	1	Uses everyday vocabulary generally appropriately (*important meeting*; *head office*), but misspelling sometimes distracts (*cluent*; *colleg*; *rellable*). The grammatical structures are mostly simple and some of the errors are noticeable (*His verry rellable*; *Please fixed*; *My colleg Andrei Ivanov go*) although meaning can still be determined.

PART TWO

- You work in the Customer Services Department of a mail-order company. You have been asked to prepare a short report for your line manager about complaints.
- Look at the information below, on which you have already made some handwritten notes.
- Then, using all your handwritten notes, write you report.
- Write 120-140 words.
- Write on the separate answer paper provided.

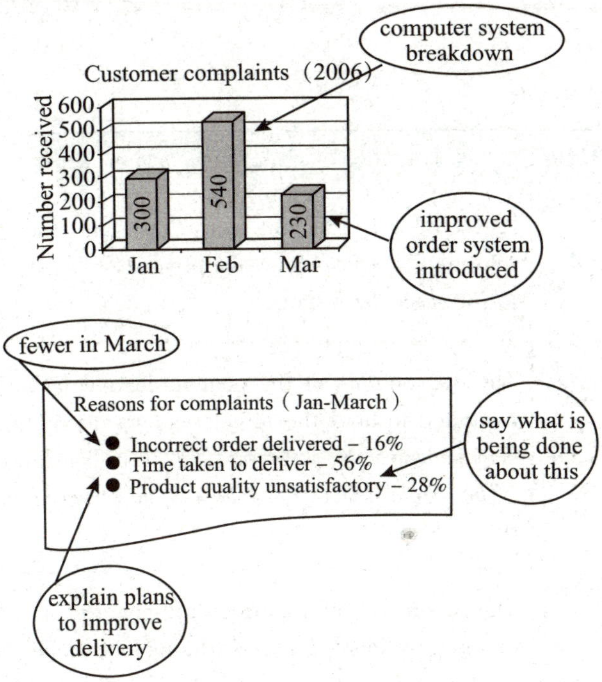

Candidate D

This report deals with the number of customer's complaints between January 2006 and March 2006 as well as with reasons for those complaints.

Complaints in January stood at 300, but in February the number rocketed to 540 because of a computer system breakdown. Finally, after introducing some improvement in the order system the number of complaints fell back to 230.

We can point out 3 main reasons for these complaints. Firstly, 10% of them were due to incorrect deliveries. In particular, March saw fewer complaints. Secondly, an excessive time for delivery led to 56% of complaints. The whole delivery system will be reviewed in order to solve the problem. Finally, 28% of complaints were due to a lack of quality in our products. This will be solved by setting up a new quality section in our process.

Examiner comments

Subscale	*Mark*	*Examiner comments*
Content	4	All content is relevant to the task and the target reader is informed. There is one slip present (10% *of them were due to incorrect deliveries*).
Communicative Achievement	5	The conventions of the communicative task have been fully exploited to hold the target reader's attention. The candidate communicates straightforward and more complex ideas effectively (*The whole delivery system will be reviewed in order to solve the problem*).
Organization	5	The report is well organised and coherent, with effective use of organisational features throughout. Cohesive devices are used appropriately (*as well as*; *in order to*; *Firstly*; *Finally*). Good use is also made of referencing (*For these complaints*; *of them*; *this will be solved*).
Language	5	Uses a range of vocabulary including less common lexis (*rocketed to*; *fell back to*; *excessive time*; *lack of*; *setting up*). Both simple and complex grammatical forms are used with control and exibility (*after introducing*; *will be reviewed*; *will be solved by*).

Candidate E

Report on 2006 first quarter's customer complaints

Introduction

The aim of this report is to give an explanation to the customer complaints.

Findings

It clearly shows that we had a peak of complaints in February (540) due to the breakdown of our computer system. Fortunately, with the introduction, in March, of an improved order system, the number came again in the average (230). The first reason for complaints (56%) is the time of delivery. In order to improve that, we decided to change our delivery company.

Furthermore, 28% of complaints results of unsatisfaction with the quality of the product, which will be resolved with the purchase of a new machine.

Finally, 16% are due to the delivery of an incorrect order. However, we pointed out fewer in March.

Conclusion

In conclusion, with all the improvements we made, the situation will be better in the futur.

Examiner comments

Subscale	*Mark*	*Examiner comments*
Content	4	Content is generally relevant to the task and the target reader would be informed. However, due to the wording of the content element related to time of delivery, the reader is not fully informed on this point.

续表

Subscale	*Mark*	*Examiner comments*
Communicative Achievement	4	Uses the conventions of the task, such as headings (*Findings*; *Conclusion*) to hold the target reader's attention effectively and to communicate both straightforward and complex ideas (*which will be resolved with the purchase of a new machine*), although occasionally a straightforward idea is not communicated effectively (*the number came again in the average* (230)).
Organization	5	The text is well organised and coherent, using a variety of cohesive devices and organisational patterns to good effect. For example, headings, referencing (*It clearly shows*; *In order to improve that*) and linking words (*In order to*; *Furthermore*; *Finally*; *However*; *In conclusion*).
Language	3	Uses a range of appropriate vocabulary, including less common lexis (*peak*; *breakdown*; *resolved*). There is a range of simple and some more complex grammatical structures (*Fortunately*, *with the introduction*, *in March*, *of an improved order system*). However, some precision of meaning is lost (*time of delivery instead of* '*time taken for delivery*'). Although errors are present (*came again in the average*; *28% of complaints results of unsatisfaction*), they do not impede communication.

Candidate F

Report

To: Rita Patel, Manager,

From:

Date: 21 November 2006

Subject: Complaints For Products

There are some problem about the mail-order supply over the period Jan-Mar 2006.

Customers complaint that there was a computer system breakdown in the month of February 2006. The number received was 540. But hopefully the improved order. Although, the number received was much less compared to the breakdown i. e. 230.

The reason for complaints have been put forward. In March 2006 16% of the products delivered were incorrect. Again the time taken for delivery was also a long term. Moreover the quality of the products being delivered are also not up to the mark i. e. 28%.

Lastly, to come across this vital problems products should be delivered on time and the quality of product needs to be good.

Examiner comments

Subscale	*Mark*	*Examiner comments*
Content	1	Some of the task has been misinterpreted (see first paragraph), leading to considerable irrelevance. The target reader would be minimally informed.
Communicative Achievement	2	Uses the conventions of the report to communicate straightforward ideas in generally appropriate ways (*There are some problem about the mail-order supply*). However, at times the reader's attention is not held due to unclear expression of ideas (*But hopefully the improved order*).
Organization	2	The text is connected and there are attempts, not always successful, to employ a variety of cohesive devices and other organisational features (*Again*; *Moreover*; *Lastly*).
Language	2	Uses appropriate everyday lexis and generally simple grammatical forms. There are some attempts at more complex language (*The number received*; *the time taken for delivery*). There are some noticeable errors although meaning can still be determined (*the time taken for delivery was also a long term*; *to come across this vital problems products should be delivered on time*).

Day 6

了解 BEC 中级写作与高级写作的异同

BEC 中级写作与高级写作在考题形式、信息点和字数要求等方面都有所不同，如下表所示：

		中级 Vantage	高级 Higher
Task 1	形式	公司内部交流	图表描述
	信息点	3 个	无固定信息点（描述要做到看文字能画出原图）
	写作注意事项	可以发挥想象，适当添加内容	忠实地描述图表，不可以自己添加信息或猜测
	字数要求	40 ~ 50 词	120 ~ 140 词
Task 2	形式	题目中给出 letter/report/proposal 中的一个	考生可以选择 letter/report/proposal 中的一个
	信息点	5 个	3 到 4 点
	写作注意事项	根据所给 notes 合理想象	题目很泛，需要考生自己在写作时补充很多信息
	字数要求	120 ~ 140 词	200 ~ 250 词

BEC 初级、中级、高级考生在写作能力上应分别能够达到以下要求：

级别	能力要求
初级	能够就给定的事实写出正式的信件 能够写出事实性质的报告 能够起草简单易懂的指令、规章等

续表

级别	能力要求
中级	能够写出用于同事间交流的便函 能够按要求完成绝大多数信件，有少量错误但不影响理解 能够写出简单的商务报告
高级	能够针对各种日常情形和正式情形为同事或对外联络提供专业服务 能够在会议上做记录，条理清晰准确 能够在工作中写出任何类型的信件

Day 7

小试牛刀：模拟测试

Model Test

PART ONE

You are the HR manager of a company. Your assistant sent you an email and asked for 3 days off to attend a seminar on team building.

- Write a replay to her：
  - saying she cannot go
  - explaining the reason
- **Write 40 – 50 words.**

To…	Lucy Huddleston
CC…	
Subject：	Team Building Seminar

PART TWO

- You are the owner of a school supply factory. A retailer has sent you a letter summarizing a recent negotiation. You have made some handwritten notes on the letter.
- Then, using **all** your handwritten notes, write a **reply** to the retailer.
- **Write 120 – 140 words.**

Dear Stewart,

It was good to see you again last week and we are delighted to inform you that Super Backpack will be included in our autumn catalogue.

Great!

As promised, listed below are the points agreed upon at the meeting.

- The contract is about the Super Backpack in three colors.

  What colors?

- You will grant us exclusive import rights for Super Backpack in China.
- The quantity will be 10,000 pieces, with a further option of 2,000.

  3,000

- The price per piece will be $15.00 for the first 10,000. You will confirm the price for optional 2,000 pieces.

  Already confirmed. $14.50

- The initial payment will be made after receiving the first batch of goods.

  before

Please let me know if further clarification is needed. I am looking forward to your written confirmation.

Best regards,

Jim Young

Chief Purchaser

Week 2

技能训练：夯实基础+改进提高

Day 1

学会变换

1. 词形变换

BEC 中级写作中会用到很多积极词汇，如常用的动词和名词，考生应该熟练运用这些词汇的变换形式。变换使用词形可以展现考生宽广的词汇域，恰当使用丰富的词形可以为作文增色。

➢积极词汇词形变换举例

(1) produce:

product, production, productive, producer, productivity

(2) employ:

employer, employee, employment

(3) compete:

competition, competitor, competitive, uncompetitive, competent

(4) consume:

consumer, consumption, consumable

(5) differ:

different, difference, differentiate

(6) distribute:

distributor, distribution, distributable

(7) respond:

response, responser, responsible, responsive

(8) receive:

receiver, reception, receptionist, receptible

（9） succeed：

success，*successful*

（10） vary：

variety，*various*，*varied*

➢词形变换练习

A. Complete the phrases with the adjectives of the words.

Example：

manager　　a __managerial__ position

（1） tradition　　a ________ company

（2） success　　a ________ firm

（3） flexibility　　a ________ labour force

（4） secretary　　________ skills

（5） strategy　　________ planning

（6） challenge　　a ________ task

（7） administration　　an ________ problem

（8） profession　　a ________ approach

B. Complete the word family table.

noun-concept	noun-people	verb	adjective	negative
competition				
advertising				
commerce				
attraction				
appeal				
consumption				
revolution				

C. Fill in the blanks with the proper words.

(1) One way of raising ______ is to reduce costs while maintaining output. (produce)

(2) Several new ______ have been taken on in the sales department. (employ)

(3) Our costs are so much higher than those of our rivals that our products are very ______. (compete)

(4) Cars, televisions and other long-lasting items are known as ______ durables. (consume)

(5) Packaging is one way of ______ one product from another. (differ)

Keys:

A. (1) traditional (2) successful (3) flexible (4) secretarial
(5) strategic (6) challenging (7) administrative (8) professional

B.

noun-concept	noun-people	verb	adjective	negative
competition	competitor	compete	competitive	non-competitive
advertising	advertiser	advertise		
commerce			commercial	non-commercial
attraction		attract	attractive	unattractive
appeal		appeal	appealing	
consumption	consumer	consume		
revolution	revolutionist	revolutionise	revolutionary	

C. (1) productivity (2) employees (3) uncompetitive
(4) consumer (5) differentiating

2. 句式变换

BEC 中级写作除要求考生具有丰富的词汇量以外，还要有多样化的语言结构。BEC 中级写作涉及的商务活动多数情况下，可以用以下句式进行描述。

➢表示原因

- due to/owing to
- because of
- as a result of
- the reason why…is…
- …is the reason why…
- …cause…to…
- …lead to…
- …result in…

➢表示结果

- as a consequence of this
- as a result
- consequently
- …mean that…

➢表示目的

- for this reason/purpose
- so that
- in order to
- so as to

➢表示解释说明

- for example/for instance
- in this case
- moreover/furthermore
- in fact
- actually

➢表示强调

- in deed
- in fact
- surely/certainly
- without any doubt
- truly/obviously
- above all

➢表示概括归纳

- in a word/in short/in brief
- on the whole
- generally speaking
- as has been stated
- finally
- in summary/in conclusion

➢表示罗列

- first, second, third
- first, then/next, after that/next, finally
- on (the) one hand...on the other hand
- besides/what's more/in addition/furthermore/moreover/another/also
- especially/in particular

➢表示时间顺序

- now/at present/recently
- after/afterwards/after that/after a while/in a few days
- at first/in the beginning/to begin with
- later, next, finally

- immediately/soon/at that moment/as soon as/the moment
- from now on/from then on
- at the same time/meanwhile
- till/not...until/before/after
- when/while/as/during

➢表示转折关系

- but/however
- while/though
- or/otherwise
- on the contrary/on the other hand/in contrast
- despite/in spite of
- except（for）/instead
- after all

➢表示并列关系

- or/and/also/too
- not only...but also
- as well as/both...and
- either...or/neither...nor

➢表示条件关系

- as（so）long as
- on condition that
- if
- unless

➢表示让步关系

- though/although/as

- even if/even though
- whether…or…
- however/whoever/whatever/whichever/wherever/whenever
- no matter how（who，what，which，where，when）

➢表示数目增加

- increase/rise/go up by
- increase/rise to
- come to/reach
- as many/high/long as
- amount to/add up to/cover to

➢表示倍数（增加）

- N times as many/much as
- N times more than
- increase N times
- N times the amount of

➢表示倍数（减少）

- reduce/decrease N times as many/much as
- N times fewer/less than
- decrease by N times

➢表示最大量、最小量和平均数

- to have the maximum/minimum of X
- the maximum speed/weight is X
- to have the highest/lowest weight limit of X
- to have an average of X
- the average length/depth/width of X is

➢与……相比

- X is much （a bit，a little，slightly，hardly，somewhat，a lot） bigger （smaller） than Y.
- With regard to…，X is better than Y.
- One of the differences between X and Y is…
- X is exactly （just，almost，nearly，more or less） the same as Y.
- X is not quite as good （big，expensive） as Y.

➢讨论优缺点

- One advantage of…is that…
- Another good thing about…is that…
- The main disadvantage of…is that…
- They also have the drawback that…

➢图表作文常用句型、句式

- It can be seen from the table/graph/diagram/chart/bar…
- As can be seen from the…
- As is shown in the…
- The above data/statistics/figures can be interpreted as follows：
- The table/chart shows/indicates/illustrates/points out the data/figures about…
- From the data presented in the table，we can conclude/make a conclusion/safely say that…
- A is nearly/almost/exactly/approximately more or less the same as B in…
- A and B are completely different in…
- Their differences and similarities lie/exist in…
- There was a very sharp/dramatic/marked/slight/small increase （drop/decline/fall） in…

Day 2

学会使用恰当的词、句、篇

1. 使用简洁的语言

BEC 中级写作要求语言简洁流畅，因此考生在写作过程中应避免拖沓、累赘重复的词句，也要避免使用极度正式或陈旧的语言。例如，下表中左栏冗长的词句（Wordy）可以改写为右栏简洁的语言（Concise）。

Wordy	Concise
There is no existing system that can do this.	No system can do this.
The regulations are provided in the booklet.	The regulations are in the booklet.
at all times	always
during the year of 1995	during 1995
in the city of Dallas	in Dallas
The problem was that the car would not start.	The car would not start.
Sign on the front of this form.	Sign this form.
Remember the fact that…	Remember…

练习

➢A 将左栏累赘重复的词语（Redundant）改成简洁的词语（Concise）

Redundant	Concise
actual experience	
a great honor and a privilege	

续表

Redundant	Concise
as a general rule	
continue on	
absolutely perfect	
first and foremost	
group meeting	
final outcome	
make a telephone call	
make contact with/get in touch with	
let me know	
make arrangements	
make a reservation	
make a booking	
give an explanation	
send an e-mail	
organize again	

➢B 将下列过于正式或陈旧的表达（Old-fashioned）改成现代语言（Modern）

Old-fashioned	Modern
I am not in a position to recommend you.	
Kindly send us the booklets.	
We deem it advisable for you to wait.	
I am sending you the price list under separate cover.	

➢C 改句练习

1. I write regarding a training course on health and safety which I attended in the month of August.

2. As you may or may not know, about 50% of jobs that come onto the market don't require a specific degree.

3. In compliance with your request, I faxed you a copy of it in the afternoon but I'm afraid some of the pages were wrong.

4. What should be the goals and objectives of the business community and the world of higher education?

5. The big company of today is not being defeated by another big company but by different varieties of small companies.

Keys:

A

Redundant	Concise
actual experience	experience
a great honor and a privilege	an honor
as a general rule	as a rule
continue on	continue
absolutely perfect	perfect
first and foremost	first
group meeting	meeting
final outcome	outcome
make a telephone call	call
make contact with/get in touch with	contact
let me know	inform
make arrangements	arrange
make a reservation	reserve
make a booking	book

续表

Redundant	Concise
give an explanation	explain
send an e-mail	email
organize again	reorganize

B

Old-fashioned	Modern
I am not in a position to recommend you.	I cannot recommend you.
Kindly send us the booklets.	Please send us the booklets.
We deem it advisable for you to wait.	We suggest you wait.
I am sending you the price list under separate cover.	I am sending you the price list separately.

C

1. I write regarding a training course on health and safety which I attended in August.

2. As you may know, about 50% of jobs that come onto the market don't require a specific degree.

3. At your request, I faxed you a copy of it in the afternoon but I'm afraid some of the pages were wrong.

4. What should be the goals of the business community and the world of higher education?

5. The big company of today is not being defeated by another big company but by varieties of small companies.

2. 使用具体信息

BEC 中级写作应使用具体的语言传递信息，切忌模糊、笼统。

英语中有一些模糊词汇如：a great deal of time，bad，large，good，small，around，old，convenient，young，little，majority，minority，most，less 等应避免使用。

例如：

Does wholesale have **a positive impact**?	Does wholesale **increase our profits**?
This will give us enough time to reach **some meaningful conclusions**.	This will give us enough time to **determine our budget**.
We **have no hesitation in advising you**…	We **advise you**…
Due to the unusual nature of the request，…	**As the request is unusual**，…

➢改句练习

1. We hope the equipment will be delivered to our company as soon as possible.
2. The preparation of new price scales is in hand.

Keys：

1. Please deliver the equipment to our company before next Friday.
2. New price scales are being prepared this week.

3. 使用合适的态度和语言风格

➢合适的态度

BEC 中级写作能够反映考生处理商务交流的能力。因此，真实的商务活动中的礼貌原则也必须体现在写作过程中。

首先，在必要时，BEC 写作中应尽量使用礼貌友好的词汇和表示感激的句式，如：

- Thank you for your letter of yesterday.
- Thank you for your prompt reply.
- Thank you for helping us in this respect.

- Thank you for your information.

其次，写作时应采用体谅对方的写作态度（You-Attitude），即尽可能考虑对方的需求，淡化“we”，强调“you”，为对方着想。例如，下表右栏“对方视角”出发的句子比左栏的句子更易让对方接受。

我方视角	对方视角
We are shipping your order on Friday.	You will receive your order by Monday, October 10.
I was pleased to hear that the project was completed.	Congratulations on successfully completing the project.

再有，BEC 写作行文时应避免使用消极性的词汇或句式，避免使用有失礼貌的言辞。例如，下表右栏的句子比左栏的句子更适合 BEC 写作。

The office is closed after four o'clock.	The office is open until four o'clock.
When I received your complaint, I checked our records.	When I received your letter, I checked our records.
The Executive Board did not receive notification.	Several members of the Executive Board inquired about the time of our December meeting. Will you please send them a follow-up?

下表中的词语，由于口气过于严厉，应尽量避免使用。

We deny your claim	We do not believe	We insist
We find it difficult to understand	We expect	We are forced
You did not say	You forgot	You neglected

续表

You failed to	You misunderstood	You must
You should know	You do not have	Your recent complaint
Your credit refusal	Your failure to	Your misunderstanding
disagreeable	confusion	impatience
incompetent	incredible	insincere
intolerable	irresponsible	irritated
objection	offensive	unbelievable

此外，有一些常用的商务英语词汇有性别歧视之嫌，在 BEC 中级写作中应稍加改变。如下表所示：

避免使用	建议使用
businessman	business person
chairman	chairperson
foremen	supervisors
salesman	sales representative/sales person
stock boy	stock clerk
workman	employee/worker

➢改句练习

1. To reduce our costs, we are changing the billing system.
2. In a company as large as ours, we seldom take an order of less than 2000 items.

Keys:

1. To provide you with clear records, we are changing our billing system.

2. Please notice that it is not our common practice to take an order of less than 2000 items.

➢合适的语言风格

BEC 中级写作主要考察的一个方面是语域（**Register**），**即在特定的语言环境下使用恰当的文体**。BEC 写作对语域的要求是：

5	语域和格式完全适当
4	语域和格式总体来说适当
3	语域和格式尚可，虽然并不完全成功
2	语域和格式不适当
1	几乎没有使用适当的语域和格式

文体主要指文章的风格是非正式（informal）、中性（neutral）、还是正式的（formal）。

➢小作文的文体与大作文的文体差异

- 小作文的语言偏重非正式或中性的风格
- 大作文一定要采用正式的语言风格

比较下面两个段落，我们可以清楚地看到非正式文体和正式文体之间的差别：

非正式文体：

> Thanks for your letter. I got it 14 Sept. I've sent a copy to comp HQ along with a memo re your financial situation. I've set a meeting for 3 Oct at 11am to talk about another bank loan. So, please let us know if you can make it a. s. a. p.

正式文体：

> Thank you for your letter received 14 September 2002. A copy has been sent to the company headquarters in addition to a memorandum concerning your financial situation. A meeting has been scheduled for 3 October 2002 at 11am to discuss your request for a further bank loan. Therefore, please inform us of your availability for this meeting at the earliest opportunity.

➢关于正式文体，还应该注意以下事项：

- 不要使用括号插入信息
- 不要缩写
- 不要引用
- 不要使用只有一个词的句子
- 不要使用口语、谚语
- 不要使用含有比喻以及其他修辞的句子

➢语域替换举例

Informal	We want to know if you've made a decision yet.
Formal	We would like to know if you have made a decision yet. We wonder if you have made a decision yet.

Informal	We should have more market research to find out the reasons.
Formal	Further market research is needed to establish the reasons. Further market research should be conducted to establish the reasons.

Informal	We hope to hold the opportunity to expand our business territory, build global reputation, and to attract more potential customers.
Formal	It is our hope to hold the opportunity to expand our business territory, build global reputation, and to attract more potential customers.

➢语域替换练习

Informal	We need to find out why customers aren't satisfied.
Formal	

Informal	We haven't improved our service, so customers are becoming fewer and fewer.
Formal	

Informal	With the technology going on, people get more and more methods to communicate with others.
Formal	

Keys:

Informal	We need to find out why customers aren't satisfied.
Formal	There is an urgent need to ascertain the reasons for customers' dissatisfaction.

Informal	We haven't improved our service, so customers are becoming fewer and fewer.
Formal	The failure to improve out service has led to a fall in the number of our customers.

Informal	With the technology going on, people get more and more methods to communicate with others.
Formal	Due to the development of technology a great number of communication methods are now available.

➢恰当运用语域风格的练习

A.

When you write a document—a memo, e-mail, fax or letter—it is important to choose the right style. One aspect of style is using the right greeting and farewell.

Match the type of document (1 – 4) with the appropriate greeting (a – d). Then choose a farewell from the following list. Some farewells may be appropriate for more than one document.

Greeting

a Dear Sir/Madam	b Dear Mr. Schulz
c Dear Jenny	d Hi Pete/Hello

Farewell

Best regards	Best wishes	Bye	Regards
See you	Yours faithfully	Yours sincerely	

type of document	greeting	farewell
1 Informal e-mail to person whom you know well		
2 Letter to a person whose name you don't know		
3 Letter to a person whose name you know		
4 Letter to a person whom you know well		

B.

When writing a document, it is important not only to use the right language, but also to choose the correct style. Below is a brief report written by Miroslav Cernik, who had an accident at his workplace. Look through the report and make any necessary improvements to the language and style.

ACCIDENT REPORT FOR HEALTH AND SAFETY DEPARTMENT

Hello. I'm Miroslav Cernik. I am a car body sprayer. I work in the paint shop. More than five years now.

It was on 14 January at 11.30, in the paint workshop. I had an accident. I was carrying materials to my workplace. Then I fell on the floor. The floor was wet. And slippery. I went to the company nurse. She treated my arm. She said, ‘It's broken. You must go home.’ I am off work now. More than one week. I am unable to help at home. I go to the physiotherapist every day. She treats me.

Please look at my claim very soon.

Keys:

A.

type of document	greeting	farewell
1 Informal e-mail to person whom you know well	d Hi Pete/Hello	Bye/See you
2 Letter to a person whose name you don't know	a Dear Sir/Madam	Yours faithfully
3 Letter to person whose name you know	b Dear Mr. Schulz	Yours sincerely
4 Letter to person whom you know well	c Dear Jenny	Best wishes/Regards/Best regards

B.

Accident report

From: Miroslav Cernik

To: Health and Safety Department

I am a car body sprayer and have worked in the paint shop for more than five years.

On 14 January at 11.30, I was working in the paint workshop when I had accident. While I was carrying materials to my workplace, I fell on the floor, which as wet and slippery. I went to the company nurse, who treated my arm. She told me that it was broken and that I had to go home.

I have been off work for more than a week. As a result of the accident I am unable to help at home. I visit the physiotherapist every day, who treats me. I would be grateful if you could investigate my claim as soon as possible.

Day 3

总结失分现象并改进提高

1. 避免照搬题目中原词原句

➢题目情景举例

Part Two

- The retail company you work for is considering installing a TV system in its store to give customers information on products and services while they shop. You have seen an advertisement for a company which provides this type of system.

➢失分段落举例

Dear Sir or Madam,

I am writing to tell you that the retail company I work for is considering installing a TV system to give customers information on products and services while they shop. I have seen an advertisement for your company which provides this type of system.

➢恰当段落举例

> Dear Sir or Madam,
>
> I am writing to enquire about your in-store television system we saw advertised in the latest edition of The Daily Mirror. We are a country-wide operating chain of sport shoe shops and are considering to provide our sales rooms with flat screens to entertain our customers and to inform them about our latest inventions.

➢三种对策

◆ 换句型

e. g.　This colour applies in every style.

There are <u>no exceptions</u> to the colour.

◆ 换同义词

e. g.　Because of a business trip, I cannot come to England at the end of November.

<u>Due to</u> a business trip, <u>I am unable to</u> come to England at the end of November.

◆ 改词性

e. g.　I would also feel pleasure to accept your offer of arranging for me to see a play in the West End.

I would also <u>be pleased</u> to accept <u>your arrangement</u> for me to see a play in the West End.

➢改写句子练习

A. 使用下划线词的动词形式改写句子

Example

We organised <u>delivery</u> of the goods for 15 September.

We delivered the goods on 15 September.

（1） The negotiation went on late into the night.

We ______________________________

（2） They sent an invoice before we received delivery.

They ______________________________

（3） We agreed a discount of nearly 15%.

The price ______________________________

（4） There was an exhibition of their products on the main stand.

They ______________________________

（5） There will be a demonstration of the new product later today.

We ______________________________

（6） Our customers showed a high level of satisfaction with our new model.

Our customers ______________________________

（7） We are going to send a replacement for the goods damaged in transit.

We ______________________________

（8） Good sales people need to learn how to give priorities to their calls.

Good ______________________________

B. 用框中的词汇改写句子

definitely	certainly	probably	certain
probable	likely	possible	unlikely

Example

More people are likely to work from home.

It's probable that more people will work from home.

（1） Mangers will definitely need very different skills to manage remote teams.

（2） With an ageing population, more people will probably work until their mid 70s.

（3） It's clear that ICT will have a dramatic effect on the way we work.

（4） I don't think the new communication technologies will make our lives easier.

（5） I think these changes may occur much more slowly than predicted.

Keys:

A. （1） We negotiated late into the night.

(2) They invoiced us before delivery.

(3) The price was discounted by nearly 15%.

(4) They exhibited their products on the main stand.

(5) We will demonstrate the new product later today.

(6) Our customers were highly/very satisfied with our new model.

(7) We are going to replace the goods damaged in transit.

(8) Good sales people need to learn how to prioritise their calls.

B. (1) Managers are **certain** to need very different skills to manage remote teams.

(2) With an ageing population, it is **probable/likely** that more people will work until their mid 70s.

(3) I think ICT will **certainly** have a dramatic effect on the way we work.

(4) In the short term, the new communication technologies are **unlikely** to make our lives easier.

(5) I think it's **possible** that these changes will occur much more slowly than predicted.

2. 避免词汇误用

➢词性错误

I wish you can consider my **suggests**. (suggestion√)

If our department wants to **success**, we must learn to reduce office cost. (succeed√)

➢用词错误

All staff must know how to **apply** a computer. (use√)

We can **touch** many new things on the internet. (have access to √)

The purpose of this letter is to **react** some opinions on the service in the dining hall. (reply to √)

➢词汇练习：选择正确用词

(1) She works for an **advertisement/advertising** agency.

(2) How will the increase in interest rates **affect/effect** your sales?

(3) My bank manager has agreed to **borrow/lend** me another $2, 000.

(4) We've had to **cancel/postpone** the meeting until next Monday.

(5) These machines are **controlled/inspected** at least once a day.

(6) My plane was **delayed/postponed** by an hour due to engine failure.

(7) Before coming here, I studied **economics/economy** at university.

(8) I am **interested/interesting** in their new camera.

(9) She applied for a **job/work** as a **personal/personnel officer/official**.

(10) Some employees have a long **journey/travel** to work every day.

(11) The cost of **life/living** has gone up again.

(12) Please send precise **measurements/measures** when ordering.

(13) We expect prices to **raise/rise** by at least five per cent.

(14) We only exchange goods if you produce a **receipt/recipe**.

(15) I must **remember/remind** the boss about that meeting this afternoon.

(16) Can you **say/tell** the difference between these two products?

(17) The company is extremely **sensible/sensitive** to any criticism.

(18) There's some more paper in the **stationary/stationery** cupboard.

Keys:

(1)	advertising	(2)	affect	(3)	lend
(4)	postpone	(5)	inspected	(6)	delayed
(7)	economics	(8)	interested	(9)	job
(9)	personnel	(9)	officer	(10)	journey
(11)	living	(12)	measures	(13)	rise
(14)	receipt	(15)	remind	(16)	tell
(17)	sensitive	(18)	stationery		

3. 避免语法误用

➢主从句叠置

× There are more and more people like to choose our company for food materials.

× There are still many problems should be noted and resolved.

√ There are more and more people **who** like to choose our company for food materials.

√ There are still many problems **that** should be noted and resolved.

➢句子成分缺失

× If sign the contract, we will surely be good partners.

√ If **we** sign the contract, we will surely be good partners.

➢语序错误

× Why we have more and more complaints from our customers?

× This graph shows clearly where have they spent the money.

√ Why **do** we have more and more complaints from our customers?

√ This graph shows clearly where **they have** spent the money.

➢时态错误

× Many people thought that the Internet will be more useful in company running.

√ Many people thought that the Internet **would** be more useful in company running.

➢语态错误

× You will ask to attend the meeting on time.

× The contract signed last month.

√ You will **be asked** to attend the meeting on time.

√ The contract **was signed** last month.

➢单复数错误

× Our supplier have the intention to raise the price by 5%.

× Please print out 50 copy of the handout for the conference.

√ Our **suppliers** have the intention to raise the price by 5%.

√ Please print out 50 **copies** of the handout for the conference.

➢非谓语动词错误

× Let me to introduce our new colleague Tony to you.

× Deliver goods on time is very important for us to get customer loyalty.

× Having worked in company for 3 years, the canteen service has changed a lot.

√ Let me ~~to~~ introduce our new colleague Tony to you.

√ **Delivering** goods on time is very important for us to get customer loyalty.

√ **While I am working** in company, the canteen service has changed a lot.

➢代词和冠词错误

× We can use computers in doing everything you like.

× A good employee should be able to do their job in an efficient way.

× Projector is an useful tool for holding conference.

√ We can use computers in doing everything **we** like.

√ A good employee should be able to do **his** job in an efficient way.

√ Projector is **a** useful tool for holding conference.

➢句子结构方面常见错误包括以下几个方面

- 并列错误

× After she came into the business, she often worked diligently and at night.

× I was told to report to the account executive and that I should bring my documents.

√ After she came into the business, she often worked diligently at night.

√ I was told to report to the account executive and bring my documents.

- 平行结构错误

× We need to train ourselves to think differently, shift our mindsets and we realize that diverse workforce open doors for us.

× Many business people choose air transportation because it is fast, offers convenience, and it is not very expensive.

√ We need to train ourselves to think differently, shift our mindsets and realize that diverse workforce open doors for us.

√ Many business people choose air transportation because it is fast, convenient and not very expensive.

- 修饰语错位

× They have the ability to work at a very sophisticated level with numbers.

√ They have the ability to work with numbers at a very sophisticated level.

- 修饰语悬垂

× Having the skills to go into the workplace, it's easy that the graduate makes a contribution right from the start.

√ Having the skills to go into the workplace, the graduate finds it easy to make a contribution right from the start.

➢语法练习

A 改写句中不恰当语法

(1) Before leaving for the airport, the time of departure should be checked on your schedule.

(2) Feeling nervous and uncomfortable, the comforting words were appreciated by the interviewees.

(3) To justify their actions, a note of explanation was sent to Mrs. Sterns.

(4) When fitted properly, you will find these new uniforms look attractive on

you.

(5) When installed completely, the supervisors will find the new machine to be time saving.

B 用单词正确形式填空

1. Our company does spend enough money on __________ (train) staff.
2. His job involves __________ (deal) with money.
3. I would be grateful __________ (get) a more responsible job.
4. __________ (advertise) on television is too expensive for my company __________ (invest) it.
5. It's not worth __________ (develop) a new product unless you know who your target customers are likely __________ (be).
6. I wouldn't risk __________ (leave) my job __________ (start) up a business on my own.
7. If the business idea is sensible, we will help __________ (develop) it by __________ (invest) money on it.
8. __________ (study) for a business degree is one of the priorities for those interested in business.

C 时态练习

Use the same verb twice in each sentence. Follow the example.

develop	be	stay	think	have

Example

As part of my job I develop new office system. Currently I'm developing a new system for processing customer complaints.

(1) Our suppliers __________ difficult about deliveries at the moment, It's strange, because usually they __________ very good.

(2) Normally on business trips to Paris we __________ in the company's flat, but it needs some repairs, so we __________ in a hotel this time.

(3) I __________ of looking for a new position, possibly in marketing, because I really __________ (not) this is the right job for me.

(4) We ___________ two sales offices in Britain. A group of visitors from the London office are here in Copenhagen now. We ___________ a reception for them in town this evening.

D 语态练习

Use the passive form of these verbs in the positive or negative to complete some extracts from a report about a trade fair.

give	run	see	send	set up	translate

(1) Staff on the stand ___________ talking to each other while visitors tried to catch their attention.

(2) On the last day of the fair customers ___________ last year's brochure because no up-to-date product literature was available.

(3) Follow-up letters ___________ to prospective customers, even though it is now over a month since the trade fair.

(4) A course in presentation techniques ___________ next month for all staff who deal with visitors at trade fairs.

(5) In the future, if we exhibit at trade fairs abroad, our product literature needs ___________ into different languages.

(6) For all trade fairs we recommend that a project team ___________ well in advance to handle all the arrangement.

E -ing 形式练习

Complete the sentences with the following verbs in the *-ing* form.

motivate	sit	complain	talk	reduce	get

(1) We are all looking forward to ___________ our Christmas bonus.

(2) ___________ the workforce is the most important factor in successful management.

(3) There's no point ___________. They are not going to change their mind.

(4) The company are considering ___________ our salaries by 5% in order to get through this tough period.

（5）She's always working on something new—she hates just __________ and __________ all day long.

Keys:

A. （1）**Before we leave** for the airport，the time of departure should be checked on **our** schedule.

（2）**Since they usually feel** nervous and uncomfortable，the comforting words were appreciated by the interviewees.

（3）A note of explanation was sent to Mrs. Sterns **in order to** justify their actions.

（4）**If these new uniforms are fitted properly**，you will find they look attractive on you.

（5）**When the new machine is installed completely**，the supervisors will find it to be time saving.

B. （1）training （2）dealing （3）to get
（4）Advertising；to invest （5）developing；to be （6）risking；to start
（7）to develop；investing （8）Studying

C. （1）are being；are （2）stay；are staying
（3）am thinking；don't think （4）have；are having

D. （1）were seen （2）were given （3）have not been sent
（4）will be run （5）to be translated （6）is/should be set up

E. （1）getting （2）Motivating （3）complaining
（4）reducing （5）sitting，talking

4. 避免标点符号误用

➢**在标点符号使用上，常出现的错误为：**

- 一逗到底，即通篇大都是逗号，很少出现句号
- 把英语里的句号“.”按汉语习惯写成“。”
- 不经意间在行文中出现很多“.”

➢英式拼写和美式拼写

在 BEC 考试中，英式拼写和美式拼写都可以，但切记全篇作文应保持一致。

- 全篇或者都是英式拼写
- 或者都是美式拼写
- 不可以二者混在一起使用

Day 4

写出准确而漂亮的句子

1. 减少句子表达错误

➢句子模糊

? Our shops remain open only eight hours a day others open twelve hours the normal business day.

? Every air-conditioner model was on display in the exhibition center stood nearby salespeople with brochures in hand.

√ **While** our shops remain open only eight hours a day, others open twelve hours the normal business day.

√ Every air-conditioner model was on display in the exhibition center, **and the salespeople** stood nearby with brochures in hand.

➢表达习惯错误

× Now 6,000 yuan can buy a P4 computer.

× A room often lives 4 – 6 students.

× I think this great change has three reasons.

× The reason for this is because some people want to have more discount.

√ Now **we** can buy a P4 computer **with** 6,000 yuan.

√ A room often **holds** 4 – 6 students.

√ I think **there are three reasons for** this great change.

√ The reason is **that** some people want to have more discount.

2. 切分过长的句子

➢过于复杂长句举例

? I should like to take this opportunity of drawing your attention to the fact that all our products are manufactured from completely natural ingredients and that we do not utilize any artificial additives whatsoever.

? We are sending you our price list and catalogue for the new season, and you will find plenty to interest you in it and will notice that every single one of our products is made from 100% natural ingredients— we use no artificial additives at all.

➢拆句练习

? I suggest that we change our service and supply fast food to give our customers what they seem to want so we can better compete with our main competitor.

√ I suggest that we change our service and supply fast food to give our customers what they seem to want. That way, we can better compete with our main competitor.

3. 改进句子过短不连贯现象

➢短句现象举例

(1) We have not raised the price. Raw materials have continued to rise.

(2) Mr. Patterson purchased three franchises. He assigned one to each of his managers.

(3) The report shows that the economy is healthy. It shows that there is no weakness in the demand of durable goods.

(4) Should Hanover Corporation accept the takeover bid? Should it explore other possible alternatives?

（5）This new computer is more than powerful. It gives access to the most up-to-date business software.

改进后：

（1）We have not raised the price **although** raw materials have continued to rise.

（2）Mr. Patterson purchased three franchises, **and** he assigned one to each of his managers.

（3）The report shows that the economy is healthy **and** there is no weakness in the demand of durable goods.

（4）Should Hanover Corporation accept the takeover bid **or** should it explore other possible alternatives?

（5）This new computer is more than powerful **because** it gives access to the most up-to-date business software.

➢合句练习

（1）The old equipment needs to be replaced. It keeps breaking down.

（2）Sharman Ltd increased its market share last year. This rose by 2%.

（3）The conference attracted new delegates. This was interesting.

（4）The company ran an advertising campaign. That's why sales rose by 10%.

（5）Effective communication involves listening to what is said. It also involves noticing what is not said.

Keys：

（1）The old equipment needs to be replaced **because** it keeps breaking down.

（2）Sharman Ltd increased its market share last year **by 2%**.

（3）**It was interesting that** the conference attracted new delegates.

（4）The company ran an advertising campaign, **and**, **as a result**, sales rose by 10%.

（5）Effective communication involves listening to what is said **and** noticing what is not said.

➢Email 改进实例：将 email 正文中短句重新组合

Dear Sir or Madam,

You put your advertisement in the September 15 issue of the *Sweater World Journal*. We have noticed the advertisement. Please send us a pamphlet of your products. Also please send us the catalogue and price-list of your products. We would appreciate it.

（此处2句可合为1句）（此处3句可合为1句）

We are a large chain of retailers. We are looking for a manufacture. The manufacture could supply us with a wide range sweaters for the adult market.

（此处3句可合为1句）

We are usually a bulk buyer. We hope you can allow us a large discount.

（此处2句可合为1句）

We are waiting for your reply soon. We look forward to hearing from you.

（此处2句重复，可删除1句）

Yours sincerely,

Tom Smith

改进后：

Dear Sir or Madam,

We have noticed your advertisement in the September 15 issue of the *Sweater World Journal*. We would appreciate it if you could send us a pamphlet of your products and the catalogue and price-list of your products.

We are a large chain of retailers and looking for a manufacture who could supply us with a wide range of sweaters for the adult market.

We are usually a bulk buyer and we hope you can allow us a large discount.

We are waiting for your reply soon.

Yours sincerely,

Tom Smith

Day 5

呈现清晰的段落结构

➢段落结构不清晰举例

Dear Mr. Wilson,

As you will remember from our telephone call, we have recently been experiencing a number of difficulties with several large customers. This has resulted in unfortunate delays in paying outstanding accounts. We are extremely sorry that your company has been affected by these developments. We are doing everything to rectify the situation. Indeed we hope to be able to settle our debts within the very near future. I would very much appreciate it if you could bear with us patiently, as I am sure that liquidation on our part would not be in your interest either.

Yours sincerely,

William Becker
Chief Clerk, Accounts

改进后：

Dear Mr. Wilson,

As you will remember from our telephone call, we have recently been experiencing a number of difficulties with several large customers. This has resulted in unfortunate delays in paying outstanding accounts.

We are extremely sorry that your company has been affected by these developments.

We are doing everything to rectify the situation. Indeed we hope to be able to settle our debts within the very near future.

I would very much appreciate it if you could bear with us patiently, as I am sure that liquidation on our part would not be in your interest either.

Yours sincerely,

William Becker

Chief Clerk, Accounts

➢段落重组练习

The following paragraphs are the reply from a magazine manager to an enquiry about advertising health products. These paragraphs are not in a logical order. Rearrange them and decide on a more logical order.

Dear Mr. White,

A The deadline for accepting copy for the October issue is 25 August.

B I enclose our media package folder for your information. This includes:

- information about our readership, analysed by gender, age, interests and purchasing preferences
- a card detailing our advertising rates
- publication dates for the next six issues of the magazine

C Please contact me if you need any further information.

D I hope you will find the information in the folder useful and relevant to your needs. As you will see, many of our readers regularly purchase food supplements.

E Thank you for your recent enquiry about advertising in our monthly magazine.

Yours sincerely,

Lucy Francis

Keys: E B D A C or E B A D C

Day 6

组织切题的内容

➢写作内容不切题包含以下几个方面：

- 插入不相干内容
- 错误理解题目情景中的业务含义
- 对要点的回答与写作目的不对应
- 不必要的寒暄

➢不相干内容举例

> I felt pleased to talk with you and your marketing team last week. John left me great impression, and so were other people. They seemed to be very capable in their job. Therefore I believe we could cooperate well.
>
> I know you are eager to get more information about the project, so I put some materials into this letter.
>
> …

此文中关于对员工的印象和对项目的合作祝愿属不相干内容，应删除。

简洁明了地说明事情可采用以下语句：

> I enjoyed meeting you and your staff last week. Here's the information you requested concerning the marketing project we discussed.

➤对要点回答不切题举例

Part One

You are the marketing manager. You won't be at the company on the meeting day you have arranged. Write an email informing the marketing team of a change of meeting date:

- inform the members a new date for a marketing meeting
- explain why the date needs to be changed
- suggest an additional point for the agenda

针对要点2，"explain why the date needs to be changed"，有些考生写道：

◆ I won't be at the company on that day, so you have to change the date.

◆ I will be doing another job at that time, so change the meeting date.

这些回答没能针对要点给出合理的具体的信息，不能算作有效回答。

切题的回答是：

…a group of important clients will come to our company

…there will be an important foreign delegation

…I won't be back from an important trade fair

…I have a training course on that day…

…we received a new task needed to be prepared as soon as possible…

针对要点3，"suggest an additional point for the agenda"，有些考生写道：

◆ please attend the meeting on time

◆ turn off your mobile phone

◆ please take your notebook

◆ confirm that the meeting will still be held in room 4

这些回答没能准确理解考点信息，不能算作有效回答。

切题的回答是：

◆ do remember to bring the quarter sales figure for discussion

◆ please bring the sales report so we can decide the sales strategy for next year

➤不切题信函举例

Your company decides to open a new branch overseas. Your line manager has asked you to contact a business advisory service:

- introduce your company
- explain your plan
- ask for advice (at least two)
- arrange a meeting

Dear Sir/Madam,

I am a staff from Nike, a famous shoe maker. Our company has decided to open a new branch in your country. We would like to know your suggestions.

To be specific, how is the weather like in your country? And secondly, can you tell me your cultures and customers? What preferences do your people have?

We would like to arrange a meeting with you so we can talk in detail. Is 10 am next Monday okay?

Thank you for your time.

Yours sincerely,

Li Ming

作为staff，不能代表自己的公司和对方通信，最好写成managing director等。

考生说自己是Nike公司的，大家可能看出这么写会给自己设置很多障碍：首先，大家都熟悉这个公司，阅卷人可以很轻松地对你的想法进行批判。其次，Nike现在可能在世界的每个角落都有自己的分支，这种海外拓展业务的计划很难自圆其说。

考生需要在信中介绍自己想在哪方面得到咨询公司的建议。有的考生思路很狭窄，说需要知道当地的风土人情、气候等。作为一个公司，当你向咨询公司咨询的时候是需要付费的，所以你必须提出既可以回答，又值得问的一些问题，最好是咨询公司需要为你而展开调查的问题，如当地的竞争对手、选址、预算等。

要求和对方面对面谈是正确的，但是在第一次写信就约定一个具体的见面时间是不现实的，可以定在下周方便的时间。

这种寒暄是完全不必要的。因为对于你所联系的咨询公司而言，你是他们的顾客，他们处理你的要求是正常的工作，所以这种寒暄没有必要。

➢排除不相干内容举例

Look at the extracts from four letters about business travel. In each letter, some phrases are missing. Choose from the phrases below to complete each text.

A. As a regular customer, I expect to receive at least an apology for the treatment I received.

B. As soon as we receive these details, we will be able to settle your claim.

C. As we have received these details, we will be able to settle you claim.

D. I am writing about your reservation for a Class B car.

E. I am writing to complain about the service provided at your hotel on 24 March.

F. My staff have informed me about the problem you experienced in your recent visit to the hotel.

G. I'm sure it won't happen again.

H. Thank you for informing us about the accident you had last week.

I. Please quote your existing booking number when you arrive.

J. I apologise for the confusion and would like to offer you free use of the facilities on your next visit.

(1)

Dear Sir/Madam,

__________ I understand that you had booked a meeting room but one wasn't available when you arrived. __________

(2)

Dear Ms Collins,

__________ We regret to inform you that we cannot process your insurance claim at present as we require further detail. __________

(3)

Dear Sir/Madam,

__________ When I tried to check in, the queue of waiting quests stretched from the lobby into the restaurant. The whole procedure took 45 minutes. __________

(4) Dear Mr Black,

____ We are pleased to be able to offer you an upgrade at no extra cost. We are sure that having a bigger car will make your journeys more comfortable and enjoyable.

____.

Keys: (1) F J (2) H B (3) E A (4) D I

Day 7

使用恰当的语体

针对不同的目标阅读人，应该使用不同的语言风格。如果是公司内部比较熟识的同事之间可以使用非正式的语言；部门之间可使用中性语言。如果是公司与公司之间的商务往来，多用正式的语体。商务报告和建议书通常用中性或正式语体。

➢语体举例

You have to go to a meeting with some suppliers next Monday.

Write an email to your assistant Sam whom you know well:

- explaining why you will be absent from the office
- saying when and how long you will be away
- requesting him to deal with customers while you are away

Write 40 – 50 words.

语言风格 1

Dear Sam,

I shall be at a meeting with our suppliers next Monday in order to discuss the new specifications for the components. As a result, I will be absent from the office for approximately two hours from 10 a. m. onwards. I would be grateful if you would attend to any customers in my absence.

Many thanks

语言风格 2

Hello Sam,

I've got a meeting with our suppliers next Monday to talk about the new specifications, so I'll be out of the office for a couple of hours from 10 – 12.

Could you deal with any customers while I'm out, please?

Thanks

因为这封电子邮件是写给非常熟悉的同事，他的助理 Sam，所以语言风格应该是非正式的，因此第二封电子邮件要好于第一封。

➢语体举例

Read the exam task below and the two sample answers. Which is the better answer? Why?

You are working late to prepare for an important meeting so will be late into work the next day. You need your assistant to carry out some tasks the following morning before you arrive.

Write a note to your assistant:

- telling her about the meeting
- asking her to call one of your customers to tell him the next delivery date
- reminding her to request provisional quantities for his next order

Write 40 – 50 words.

Sample note 1

I am delayed because I have been working very late last night. I need you to help me with these things:

—Call Mr. Kendall telling him that his delivery will arrive next Friday.

—Ask to our supplier to send us another lot of the AXB item for the next order.

Sample note 2

Maria,

I have been working late to prepare for this afternoon meeting so I will be late in the morning. Could you call Mr. Anderson and inform the next delivery will be made on Friday? Please, don't forget to check provisional quantities for the order we have to deliver next week.

Thanks

R. B.

Keys：Note 2 is better.

Note 1 （suggested mark：7/10）

- doesn't mention the meeting
- errors：**I was delayed because I was working** or the time reference （*last night*） needs to be dropped；**Ask our supplier**
- style/content：generally appropriate，but *another lot of* is too colloquial

Note 2 （Suggest mark：9/10）

- all points covered
- errors：this **afternoon's** meeting；inform **him**
- style/content：excellent and appropriate

Week 3

逐项突破（1）：PART ONE 公司内部商务往来写作解析

Day 1

了解写作任务

1. 任务指导语（input）分析

BEC 中级考试中 PART ONE 要求考生写一份 40 ~ 50 字的电子邮件、备忘录或便条。PART ONE 的写作目的是用于公司内部交流，给出的任务指导语通常包含以下六个方面：

<table>
<tr><th>任务指导语内容</th><th>例句</th></tr>
<tr><td>✧情景描述</td><td rowspan="2">You work for MK Precision. The order from Visionone for two fog-lights arrived damaged. Your boss, Sharon Silverman, asked you to contact Yolanda Anderson at Visionone to find out what happened.</td></tr>
<tr><td>✧写作人身份</td></tr>
<tr><td>✧目标阅读人身份</td><td rowspan="3">Write an email to your boss to summarize your conversation:
• giving Yolanda's explanation—damaged during transport
• telling her Yolanda will contact delivery service, Air Parcel Post, for an explanation
• informing her of Yolanda's solution—send replacement direct to Mr. Jackson, the customer, by courier</td></tr>
<tr><td>✧答题要点（3 点）</td></tr>
<tr><td>✧答题形式</td></tr>
<tr><td>✧字数要求</td><td>Write 40 – 50 words.</td></tr>
</table>

2. 三种常用答题形式 Email，Memo & Note

PART ONE 三种常见的答题形式是

- Email

- Memo
- Note

为表现考题情景的真实性，考试时会事先给定其中一种形式让考生答题，并且给出基本信息。考生不需考虑格式框中收信人、日期、主题等细节。

Email

To…	Sharon Silverman
CC…	
Subject：	Conversation

Memo

Memo	
To：	Linda Johnson
From：	Susan Smith
Subject：	Marketing meeting

Note

NOTEPAD
To：Lucy From：Nick

Day 2

熟悉书写格式

1. Email，Memo，Note 的书写格式

一般说来，这三种形式的书写格式比较相近，都包括收信人姓名、正文、结束语和署名这四个要素。在 BEC 中级考试中，由于格式框中已包含一些基本信息，考生可灵活处理书写格式，并根据题目情景中写信人和收信人的关系，确定合适的语气，使用恰当的表达方式。

内容要素	表达方式
收信人 下级（assistant/secretary） 同级（...manager） 全体同事（All staff/team）	可选择不写 Dear + given name Dear + Mr. /Mrs. + family name Dear colleagues
正文	
结束语	可选择不写 Thanks/Many thanks/Thank you Kind regards Regards Please reply soon Please accept my apologies …
署名	可选择不写 名（Given name） 全名（Full name）

2. 使用名字时的注意事项

- 如果任务中涉及到接受人或发起人名字，则使用该名字
- 如果需要编写名字，则使用常见男性名字或女性名字
- 按英语姓名习惯使用常见的名（Given name）和姓（Family name）
- 用全名或全名的缩写形式，如 Susan Smith 或 S. Smith
- 一般不使用尊称，如果写给上级，可加上尊称甚至职位，例如 Mr. Tom Gates – Managing Director
- 写 note 时，一般只写接受人和发起人的名（Given name）不需要写姓（Family name）

3. 目标阅读人身份分析

BEC 中级写作对 PART ONE 的语域要求是非正式或中性，准确分析目标阅读人的身份有利于选择使用恰当的语言风格。考生可以根据发起人和接受人的关系以及写作内容判断语气的正式程度。

考虑要素	目标阅读人身份	语言风格
级别	上级	中性
	下属	非正式/中性
	同级其他部门管理人员	中性
人数	一个人	非正式/中性
	小组成员	中性
	全体员工	中性

非正式语言并不意味不礼貌，正式语言也不代表语气生硬。总之行文时要根据情景提示，做到语言简洁明了，不让目标阅读人反感。

Day 3

掌握写作方法（三句写作法）

1. 三句写作法的含义

PART ONE 任务要求考生结合情景，回答三个要点。考生的写作内容既要简要提及任务情景，又要回答三个要点。因此通常情况下，考生的写作内容要体现以下三种功能：

- 告知事由
- 扩充信息
- 强调或补充

考生在考虑写作内容时可以从这三个功能出发，组句成段，即三句写作法。需要注意的是，因为词数要求有限，且三个句子已经紧扣答题要点，所以行文时要尽量避免使用“first”和“second”之类的过渡词语。

第一句	告知事由 计划打算 事件 人物 时间 地点 ……
第二句	扩充信息 解释原因 说明重要性 交待具体信息 询问 ……

续表

第三句	强调或补充 建议 要求 希望 补充信息 ……

2. 三句写作法举例

You are an HR Manager. You are responsible for introducing an incentive scheme to motivate the workforce. Before the programme starts, you want to get some reactions to your ideas from the rest of the management team.

Complete the memo below:

- mentioning the three options—Christmas bonus, performance bonus, profits share
- asking for their opinions
- giving a deadline for their feedback

The memo should be 40 – 50words in total.

例文：

As you all know, we are planning to introduce a new staff incentive scheme and there are three options to consider: Christmas bonus, performance bonus and profits share. I would be interested to know what you think about these options. Please let me have your feedback by 15 June.

三句写作法的步骤：

第一句　告知事由	As you all know, **we are planning to** introduce a new staff incentive scheme and there are three options to consider: Christmas bonus, performance bonus and profits share.
第二句　询问	**I would be interested** to know what you think about these options.
第三句　希望	**Please** let me have your feedback by 15 June.

需要注意的是第三句如果要求补充信息，很有可能是对第二句的扩展。例如：

> Peter Brown is the store manager of Global Computers, a retailer of PC equipment in Brentwood. He has ordered some PCs from his distribution center in Brussels, which have not arrived yet.
>
> Write an email of 40 – 50 words to Monica de Vries, the Customer Relations Manager:
>
> - pointing out that the order (IF435) was made six weeks ago and promised within four weeks
> - saying that he urgently needs to supply the customers
> - explaining why it is urgent

例文：

> Dear Monica,
>
> The order of IF435 was placed six weeks ago and I was guaranteed delivery within a maximum of four weeks. This is now urgently required as I have customers waiting for their order. If I don't get the goods to them as soon as possible, they will take their business elsewhere.

三句写作法的步骤：

第一句　告知事由	The order of IF435 was placed six weeks ago and I was guaranteed delivery within a maximum of four weeks.
第二句　说明重要性	This **is** now **urgently required as** I have customers waiting for their order.
第三句　补充信息	**If** I don't get the goods to them as soon as possible, they **will** take their business elsewhere.

Day 4

熟记常用句式

三句写作法有助于考生简洁明了地说明答题要点内容，展现考生组织衔接语句的能力。写第一句时，应该直接进入主题，避免寒暄和问候等客套；写第二句扩充信息时，可以使用商务常用表达句式，显得比较专业；写第三句时，要根据语境，注意语气。

➢第一句告知事由常用句式

- I'm writing to inform you that...
- I would like you to know...
- I'm pleased to inform you that...
- I would like to inform you that...
- You'll be pleased to learn that...
- This is to let you know that...

- ...has given me the information...
- I received an email from...
- I have learnt that...
- ...told me that...
- Recently...

- We're going to...
- Based on..., we are going to...
- We're introducing... (scheme/program) ...on (*time*)...
- We're interested in...

- To support/improve..., ...is needed/required to...

- （The board） urgently requires/needs…（to be done）…
- The trip/meeting has been confirmed for（*time*）…

➢第二句扩充信息常用句式

解释原因

…is needed because…

…I cannot…because…

（The dissatisfaction） is due to/owing to…

The reason why…is…

…is the reason why…

…lead to…

…result in…

说明重要性

If we…， we will…

It will improve…if we…

…is of great importance in…

交待事项

Your suggestions concerning…are welcome.

Since…， we are required to/have to

Please（do）…

询问

Could you please let me know…

I would like you to tell me…

Please tell me…

Please let me know…

➢第三句强调或补充常用句式

建议

I suggest…

We are recommending...

要求

...is expected to finish by（*time*）...

Please（do）...before...

All...staff are,（on receiving this email）, required to（comply with the regulations）...

希望

I hope...will lead to...

补充信息

Please also remember to/tell...to...

Day 5

攻克写作难点（1）：转述任务

PART ONE 写作要求的字数比较少，只有 40 ~ 50 词。如果考生在短文中完全或大部分照抄题目情景和内容要点中的词句，则不能体现考生自己的商务英语写作能力。因此，可采用换句型、换同义词、改词性等三种方法，变化语句说明要点，再补充相应信息充实段落内容。如果不知道如何变化，或没有把握，至少要把要点补充为完整的句子。例如：

You are Sales Manager at Caramia in Holland. You are planning a team-building seminar for your sales team. Katie Whitely, a colleague at your company's Head Office in Dublin has given good reports about a company called CFI Training.

Write an email of 40 – 50 words to Katie:

- asking her to contact Kevin Lynch at CFI Training to find out if he could run the seminar for 30 people in July
- informing her that you need his proposal by Friday
- suggesting Kevin telephones you at 9 a. m. tomorrow to find out more

例文：

Could you ask Kevin Lynch at CFI Training about running a team-building seminar for 30 of our sales staff in July? If he is interested, tell him it's urgent and I need his proposal by Friday. He can contact me tomorrow at nine for more details.

原词句与变化的词句对比：

原词句	变化的词句
Write an email of 40 – 50 words to Katie: ● asking her to **contact** Kevin Lynch at CFI Training to find out if he could run the seminar for **30 people** in July ● informing her that you need his proposal by Friday ● suggesting Kevin **telephones** you at 9 a. m. tomorrow **to find out more**	Could you **ask** Kevin Lynch at CFI Training **about** running a team-building seminar for **30 of our sales staff** in July? If he is interested, tell him it's urgent and I need his proposal by Friday. He can **contact** me tomorrow at nine **for more details**.

Day 6

攻克写作难点（2）：合理扩充要点

PART ONE 的三个答题要点是以动名词短语形式给出的，每个短语中的关键词都有一定的扩展空间，例如解释原因、交待工作内容等。考生在三句写作法的基础上，需要结合相关的商务知识，进行合理发挥，完成所指定的三项任务。合理发挥的原则是切题、真实、可行、具体。

例如：

You are the Managing Director of a company whose profits have recently increased and you would like to reward staff for this.

Write an email to all staff：

- thanking them for their contribution
- explaining why profits increased
- telling them what their reward will be

Write 40 – 50 words.

例文：

To：All Staff

From：Bill Bush

Date：7 December 2002

Subject：Staff Reward

The profits of our company this month went up 10% compared with the same period last year owing to your hard work and long working hours. I would like to thank you for your long devoted service. A trip to Hawaii has been arranged next month as a prize. Enjoy!

这个写作任务的情景中提到公司利润增长，并要求回答三个答题要点，分别是：

- 感谢员工
- 解释利润增长原因
- 宣布奖励

针对要点展开论述时，可以考虑利润增长的原因可能是销售量增加（the increase of sales）、成本降低（the reduction of cost）或推出新产品（the launch of the new product）；而奖励的内容可以是集体旅行（a company trip）、涨工资（an increase of salary）或发放奖金（bonus）。

扩充要点时应注意两点：第一，要体现具体信息，比如利润的增长比上年同时段增加 10%；其二，扩展内容应符合商务实际，如全体员工工资上浮 50%、增加带薪假期（paid leave）、开派对（a party）或唱卡拉 OK（Karaoke）等奖励都是不符合商务实际的。如果对商务实务不熟悉，可用简单的理由以避免出错，比如公司业绩增长的原因可以宽泛地写成是员工的努力工作和加班（hard work and long working hours）。

Day 7

写作注意事项

PART ONE 主要考查考生按照题目要求完成任务的能力，组织衔接观点的能力，语言表达的得体性，词语的丰富性，语法、拼写的准确性等。因此，答题过程中要注意以下事项：

注意事项	是否做到
直接进入主题，避免客套	√
语言简洁紧凑	√
转述任务情景	√
合理扩充要点内容	√
语域恰当	√
避免拼写及语法错误	√
字数在 40～50 词以内	√

Week 4

逐项突破（2）：PART TWO商务信函写作解析

Day 1

了解写作任务

1. 商务信函与商务便函及便条的比较

商务信函写作与商务便函及便条写作的差别主要体现在以下四个方面：

- 读者不同

  信函的目标读者一般是公司外部的人员，而便函及便条的目标读者为公司内部人员。

- 答题要点数量不同

  就考题而言，二者的答题要点数量不同，小作文的要点通常为三个，而大作文的要点为五个。

- 阅读量不同

  与小作文相比，大作文的阅读量要大很多，至少需要读一封信，有些情况还需要读两封。

- 字数要求不同

  小作文要求作文字数为 40～50 词，而大作文则为 120～140 词。

2. 商务信函题目分类

这一题型要求考生根据所提供的短文，如书信、传真、便函、留言条（电话留言条）等，起草一封书信，字数要求达到 120～140 词。

题目结构一般为：

已知信息：（1）场景描述（situation description）

（2）写作任务（task）

（3）目标读者（target reader）

阅读材料：便条、信件、传真及内容要点（texts in note，letter，fax or memo and content points）

写作任务：一封 120 ~ 140 词的信函（a business letter of 120 – 140 words）

根据题目类型，可将此类作文分成四大类：

- 订单类（handling order）
- 询问类（enquiry and reply）
- 投诉类（complaint and apology）
- 告知变化类（notice of changes）

Day 2

熟悉写作格式

商务信函的格式有两种：平头式和缩进式，考生可根据自己的习惯进行选择。

Block Version（平头式）

Dear Sir or Madam, We're writing in connection with… We enclose a quotation for summer wares, … Yours faithfully, Edward White

Indented Version（缩进式）

Dear Sir or Madam,
 	
    Thank you for…
    …
 	
Yours faithfully,
 	
John Black

➢常用称呼和结束礼词

常用称呼语：

Dear Sir or Madam	写信给某一公司，不确定具体的收信人
Dear Sir	对男士，但是不知道他的具体姓名
Dear Madam	对女士，但是不知道她的具体姓名
Dear Mr. Smith	对男士
Dear Ms. Smith	对已婚或未婚的女士
Dear Mrs. Smith	对已婚女士
Dear Miss Smith	对未婚女士
Dear John（此处 John 为英语中常用男名）	对朋友或你比较熟悉的人（通常为多年生意伙伴）

称呼与结束礼词的对应关系：

Dear Sir or Madam	Yours faithfully
Dear Mr. /Ms. /Mrs. /Miss Smith	Yours sincerely
Dear John	Best wishes

➢日期的写法

- 在英国英语中，日期的表示方法为：日、月、年
- 在美国英语中，则为：月、日、年
- 例如：2017 年 5 月 6 日，用英国英语表示为：6/5/2017，用美国英语表示则为：5/6/2017
- 为避免误解，日期要用完全形式书写，应写成：6 May 2017 或 May 6, 2017

Day 3

掌握写作步骤

步 骤	注意事项
（1）认真审题，明确写作目的	不要忽略题目里每一个信息
（2）按照重要程度罗列内容要点	不要有所遗漏，也要避免出现与主题不相干的内容
（3）列出提纲	文章的结构应清晰、自然
（4）完成初稿	书写应整齐规整，易于辨认
（5）检查	完成初稿后，从以下方面进行自查： * 布局是否合理 * 拼写是否正确？标点符号用得是否恰当 * 是否包含所有要点？所传递的信息是否准确 * 措辞是否简明、准确、礼貌 * 语言是否自然、真诚 * 是否做到从对方角度出发，体谅对方 * 全文总基调是否合适？能否产生预期的效果

Day 4

例题与解析（1）

1. 订单类信函写作

PART TWO

* You are the owner of a toy factory. A customer has sent you a letter summarising a negotiation made a week ago. You have written some notes on the letter.
* Write a 120 – 140 words reply to the buyer using the letter and your notes.
* Write on your Answer Sheet.

Mrs. C Carabott
Watt Toys
20 Granada Road
Portsmouth

Dear Clare,

It was good to see you again last week and we are delighted that your toys will be included in our summer catalogue. [note: so are we!]

As promised, listed below are the points agreed at the meeting.
The contract is for the Ella range of toys in three styles. [note: which styles?]
You will grant us exclusive import rights for the toys in the UK.
The quantity will be 10,000 pieces, with a further option of 4,000. [note: we agreed 5,000?]
The price per piece will be $2.55 for the first 10,000. You will confirm the price for the optional 4,000 pieces. [note: $ 2.35 for the option pieces]
Payment will be by letter of credit.

> The initial order will be ready ex factory by 1 October 2009.
>
> I trust you will find this in order. I look forward to your written confirmation in due course.
>
> [not possible —15th at the earliest]
>
> Best regards
>
> Paul Johnson
>
> Chief Purchaser

从题目可以看出，回信需包括五个内容点，其安排需仔细考虑。若都放入一个自然段，会显得杂乱。因此我们把它们分成三部分加以说明，分别为第一、二、三自然段，这样整个文章浑然一体，层次清晰。

例文：

> Dear Paul,
>
> Thank you for your letter of 3 April concerning our negotiation. We are delighted that the Ella range will be in your catalogue.
>
> There are, however, some small points which need clarifying.
>
> - The Ella range comes in six styles. Please look at the samples and confirm which three styles you would like.
> - You referred to the further option of 4,000 pieces. I thought we had agreed on 5,000. Please check the correct figure.
> - I can confirm the optional pieces will cost $2.35 each.
>
> With reference to the delivery date, we regret to tell you that we are unable to deliver by 1 October 2009. The earliest date would be 15 October 2009. I hope this will be acceptable for you.
>
> Please feel free to contact me if you have any further questions.
>
> Yours sincerely,
>
> Clare Carabott

作者首先对对方来信表示感谢，然后覆盖第一个内容点：很高兴对方订购我们的货物，过渡自然，不留痕迹。接下来，作者笔锋一转（however），说明有些问题需要澄清，引出其他三个内容点，各点以并列的形式加以展现，清晰自然。作者用“With reference to the delivery date”顺利引出最后一个要点，衔接自然，不突兀。文章结尾是商务信函的常用套路，借此表示诚意。

2. 询问类信函写作

PART TWO

* You are an advertising sales assistant at DIY Round-up magazine. Your boss has passed you the letter below and asked you to reply to it.
* Look at the letter and the hand-written notes your boss has made on it. Then using all these notes, write your letter.
* Write 120 – 140 words.

RED TIGER TOOLS

RED TIGER TOOLS
PO Box 11734
London
WC1 6PP

Advertising Sales Manager
DIY Round-up Magazine
PO Box 653
Bath BA1 2 AA

Point out that ours are more than 60% DIY enthusiasts and the rest small business owners (joinery, construction, etc)

Dear Sir or Madam,

We are a Korean company which produces power drills and other hand-held tools. Our European customers are mainly DIY enthusiasts and small businesses in the construction trade.

We are launching a new lightweight power drill in the UK market later this year and may be interested in placing a series of advertisements in your DIY Round-up magazine.

Could you please send me information about the readership of your magazine and your advertising rates for different sizes and styles of ads?

Yours faithfully,

Vickie Moon
Assistant to the UK Sales Manager

Send our usual 'ad kit' (statistics about our readers, advertising rates card, current issue of the magazine)

Send some examples from former issues, she may find this helpful

回信需注意三个内容点之间的衔接，这样可以使文章结构紧凑、不松散，内容完整、连贯。

例文：

Dear Vickie Moon,

Thank you for your letter enquiring about doing advertisements in our magazine.

I am delighted to inform you that our readers include more than 60% DIY enthusiasts and the rest are the owners of small businesses in joinery, construction and so on.

With reference to the readership and advertising rates of our magazine, you will get the corresponding information from the usual "ad kit" enclosed, which consists of the statistics of our readers, our advertising rates card and the current issue of the magazine.

Further to the "ad kit", we are sending you some examples from former issues, which I hope might be helpful.

We look forward to cooperating with you and please do not hesitate to contact us if you need any further information.

Yours sincerely,

…

作者将文章分成若干段落，每一个段落覆盖一个要点，各段落之间使用不同的关联词衔接（With reference to…, Further to…），层次清晰。在每一段落中，句与句之间的衔接也得体、恰当。

Day 5

例题与解析（2）

1. 投诉类信函写作

PART TWO

* You work for a wine merchant. You have been asked to write a reply to a customer complaint.
* Look at the letter on which you have already made some notes. Then using all your notes, write your letter.
* Write 120 – 140 words.

10 Neverwindings
Salisbury
Wiltshire
14 June

Apologise and express surprise

Apologise for the late delivery, due to enormous demand

Dear Sir,

I recently responded to the special offer advertised in the national press. I filled in the order form six weeks ago and paid by credit card.

The case of wine finally arrived yesterday and I celebrated by opening the first bottle. It was a major disappointment as it tasted sour.

I certainly do not want to risk opening any further bottles and would like you to reimburse for the full cost.

Enclose a voucher for the full value of the order

Yours faithfully,

Paul Gillford

Enclose latest catalogue — hope to receive new order

该作文的难点是作者需要对其中两点进行道歉并解释原因，措辞应诚恳，条理要清晰。

例文：

Dear Mr. Gillford,

We are writing in connection with your letter of June 14. We are extremely sorry for the delay at the delivery, but we had a big demand of cases at the time.

We were very surprised when we heard about the bottle of wine with bad taste. It is the first time that this has happened in our company. We apologise for this and we are sure this will never happen again.

In reference to the cost of the original case, we are sending to you a voucher for the full value of the order. Also we enclose the latest catalogue with new products and special offers. We hope to receive a new order from you.

Please contact us if you need any further information and we look forward to receiving your new order.

Yours sincerely,

Philippen Deval

作者首先向对方表示歉意，然后解释事情发生的原因，最后提出解决办法并表示以后不会发生类似事情。措辞合理，态度诚恳。

2. 告知变化类信函写作

PART TWO

* You work in the Sales Department of an international company. Connie White, an important client, is visiting your company for a day. There are some changes to the itinerary you sent her last week.
* Write a letter of 120 – 140 words to Ms. White, using the original itinerary and your handwritten notes, informing her of the changes.

* Do not include addresses.
* Write on your answer sheet.

Proposed itinerary for one-day visit of Connie White

Wednesday 15 September

10:00 Ms. White arrives on flight K838 from Singapore
John Smith to meet Ms. White at airport

10:30 Arrival at company [original arrival time too optimistic]
John Smith to give Ms. White an introductory tour of company

11:30 Lunch at White Hart restaurant [restaurant full. It's now the Swan hotel]
(John Smith, Carol Snape, Sue Smith, Tom Brown, Connie White) [Carol can't make it, explain why]

13:30 Meeting in boardroom
(Carol Snape, Sue Smith, Tom Brown, Connie White)

14:30 Coffee break

14:50 Product presentation [give some details]
(Carol Snape, Sue Smith, Tom Brown, Connie White)

16:30 John Smith to take Ms. White to the airport [John has to go early. Sue will take Connie to the airport]

17:40 Ms. White departs on flight R886 to Singapore

该信件需告知对方四个变化和产品展示的细节，措辞应得体、礼貌，切忌生硬。同时应合理安排各内容点，使文章结构清晰。

例文：

Dear Ms. White,

Further to last week's correspondence, I am writing to inform you that we have to make a few changes to the original itinerary for Wednesday 15 September.

In order to allow plenty of time for you to travel from the airport, your tour of the company will be slightly shorter than the hour which we had originally planned. In addition, please note that lunch will be at the Swan Hotel as the White Hart is full on Wednesday. However, Carol Snape will not be joining us due to a previous engagement.

It has been confirmed that Tom Brown will show the sample of the new-style blouse at 14:50. As John Smith has to leave early, Sue Smith will accompany you to the airport for your evening flight.

Please feel free to contact me if you have any further questions.

Yours sincerely,

…

作者开门见山，告诉对方写信目的。在第二自然段，作者告知对方三个变化，衔接恰当；在接下来的段落里，作者介绍了产品展示的情况和第四个变化。文章层次清晰，信息传递准确。

Day 6

样题、例文及点评

PART TWO

* You work for Business Space plc, a company which rents fully serviced offices to other businesses. You have just received the fax below.
* Look at the fax and the other information below, on which you have already made some handwritten notes.
* Then, using all your handwritten notes, write a fax in reply to Rwinhard Mieter.
* Write 120 – 140 words.

RENVER ESTATES

Fax

To: BusinessSpace
From: Reinhard Mieter
Subject: Renting Office Space

Further to our discussion last week we have now decided to rent office space from you for the next twelve months:

(offer 10% discount for 18-month booking)

Requirements

- one office of 10 m, two of 15 m, one of 20 m
- must be on the same floor
- 40 parking spaces

Please confirm if this office space is vacant in Central Tower.

CENTRAL TOWER (CT)	
Office currently vacant	Size m
CT 19	10
CT 24	20
CT 53	15
CT 54	15

four left, different floors, no parking — suggest Opera Place

OPERA PLACE (OP)	
Office currently vacant	Size m
OP 34	10
OP 39	20
OP 46	10
OP 47	15
OP 48	20
OP 49	15

four same floor

OPERA PLACE

Why choose Opera Place?

- 300 parking spaces
- good public transport connections
- wonderful views

mention these benefits

回信应包括以下内容要点：

- 若对方租期为 18 个月，可以九折优惠
- 在 Central Tower 里，没有满足对方要求的办公室：楼层不同，无停车位置
- 建议对方租用 Opera Space 里面的办公室
- 解释原因：同一楼层，300 个停车位，交通便利，风景优美

考生应合理安排内容要点，注意每个要点之间的衔接，使文章表达清楚、层次清晰。

Candidate A

Dear Mr. Mieter,

Thank you for your order by fax. I'd like to mention that I can offer you 10% discount if you are booking for 18-month period.

We have 4 offices left in Central Tower as you required but they are on different floors. Also there is no parking space available at the moment in Central Tower. I can offer you a very interesting alternative in Opera Place Building:

* 4 offices as you required on the same floor
* 300 parking spaces and good public transport connections for your employees
* wonderful views

Please think about this alternative and the discount I mentioned before. I look forward to hearing from you soon so I can make the booking.

Yours sincerely,

...

得分：5 分

- 所有内容点都已包括在内

作者在首段提及第一个内容要点，其余内容要点在文章主体段落第二段提及。

- 语言规范、自然，无错误

作者有很强的语言表达能力，文章语言流畅，一气呵成。

- 词汇量丰富

作者使用了“as you required”“available”“alternative”等词语。

- 条理清晰，注意前后呼应

文章层次清楚，过渡自然。最后一段作者强调“Please think about this alternative and the discount I mentioned before”，和文章首段呼应。

Candidate B

Dear Mr. Mieter,

Thank you for your fax. And we are glad you have decided to rent office space from us for the next twelve months. I'd like to inform you that we can offer 10% discount for 18-month booking, please confirm whether you'll book longer or not.

As requested we couldn't supply you in Central Tower, since there is no vacancy on the same floor and no parking either. But I recommend Opera Place, a suitable place as well. There are four in the same floor, and the sizes are poorer. 300 parking spaces are there, which is enough for you. Moreover, public transport connections here are good as well as wonderful views. I hope this change will be convenient for you. Meanwhile, I am sure you will be satisfied with Opera Place.

I'm looking forward to hearing from you.

Sincerely yours,

…

得分：3 分

- 所有内容要点都已包括在内
- 语言有错误，但不妨碍理解

文章语言略显啰唆，而且有一些错误，如：

As requested we couldn't supply you in Central Tower.

300 parking spaces are there, which is enough for you.

Moreover, public transport connections here are good as well as wonderful views.

- 结构较合理，组织效果尚可

作者在文章第二段使用多个起连接作用的词或短语，如："since" "but" "moreover" "as well as"，"meanwhile" 等，略显混乱。

Day 7

熟记常用句型及表达

1. 商务信件常用表达

Request
We got your address from…
Your advertisement has come to our attention.
We were told that you produce…
We intend to buy…/We are considering the purchase of…
We have a steady demand for…
We would like to know more about…
Could you please send us information about…?
Please send us your catalogue.
Offer
We are pleased to hear that you are interested in our products.
We hereby send you our offer.
Enclosed please find our offer. /Enclosed you will find our offer.
We are pleased to make the following offer：
We assure you that your order will be dealt with promptly.
Please let us know your requirements as soon as possible.
We look forward to receiving your order.

续表

Order
Enclosed please find our order. /Our order is enclosed.
We would like to place the following order:
We herewith order the following items:
We require the goods urgently.
We would be grateful if you could deliver as soon as possible.
Please let us know when we can expect the delivery.
Dispatch Note
We are pleased to inform you that your goods were sent today.
We hereby inform you that your goods will be delivered tomorrow.
We hope that the goods will arrive in perfect condition.
We look forward to doing business with you again.
Acknowledgement of Receipt
We have received your delivery.
Your delivery arrived in perfect condition on…
Thank you very much for executing our order professionally.
Invoice
Please find enclosed invoice…for…
Thank you for your order.
We look forward to doing business with you again.
Reminder
According to our records, we have not yet received a remittance for above invoice.
May we remind you that your payment is overdue for three months.
This is to remind you that above invoice is still unpaid.
We would appreciate if you cleared your account within the next days.
Please send your payment promptly.
If you have already sent your payment, please disregard this letter.

2. 商务信件常用句型结构及举例

信件的开头：

句型
• We are writing in connection with…
• We are writing to enquire about…
• We are interested in…and we would like to know…
举例
We are writing to enquire about the prices of some vacuum cleaners.
We are writing in connection with the advertisement in the newspaper yesterday.

回信的开头：

句型
• Thank you for your letter of（date）asking if…/enquiring about…
• We have received your letter of（date）enclosing…/concerning…
举例
We have received your letter of 8 October，enclosing your curriculum vitae.
Thank you for your fax of 13 July，asking if I was going to the marketing conference in New York.

信件的结尾：

句型
• I look forward to receiving your reply/order/products/etc.
• Looking forward to hearing from you.
• I hope that this information will help you. • Please let me know if you need any further information.
举例
Please contact me if you need any further information.
Please feel free to contact me if you have any further questions.

引入主题：

句型
• With reference to…
• Further to…
• With regard to…
• I am writing in connection with…
举例
Further to the meeting on 17 February, I am delighted to tell you that we are now able to give you a special offer for our printers.
I am writing in connection with your application for a post as secretary in our company.
With reference to your fax order for six computers, I regret to tell you that they are out of stock at present.

告知好、坏消息：

句型
• I am pleased/delighted/happy to tell/inform/advise you that…
• I regret/am sorry to tell/inform you that…
• We regret that…
举例
I am pleased to inform you that your photocopying machine has been repaired.
We regret to tell you that we have been forced to cut all salaries by 10%.

说明你所能做的和不能做的：

句型
• We are unable to…
• We are able to…
举例
We are able to give you a discount of 5% if your order is more than $ 8,000.
We are sorry that we are unable to accept payments in Egyptian pounds but we are able to accept US dollars or Euros.

说明原因：

句型
• This is owing to…(owing to the fact that…) /due to…(due to the fact that…)
• This is the result of…/because of…(because that…)

续表

举例
We are able to increase all salaries by 10%. This is the result of a big rise in sales.
We have been forced to cancel the meeting. This is due to the fact that some members of our staff have been ill.

请求采取行动：

句型
• We would be grateful if you could...as soon as possible.
• We would appreciate it if you could...without delay. /immediately.
举例
We would be grateful if you could send a repairman to fix our printer as soon as possible.
We would appreciate it if you could install another telephone in our office without delay.

道歉：

句型
• We （must） apologize for/that...
• We are extremely sorry for/that...
• Please accept our apologies once again.
• We hope that this has not caused you any inconvenience.
举例
We must apologize that our repairman didn't go to your office as promised.
We are extremely sorry for our delay of two days in shipment.

要求提供信息：

句型
• We would be grateful/appreciate it if you could give us further details about…
• We would like to know（about/if）…
举例
We would be grateful if you could let us know if the letter has reached you.
In particular，I would like to know your flight number，date and time of arrival.

抱怨：

句型
Unfortunately，something is wrong…
举例
Unfortunately，you sent us a bill for the wrong goods. Please send us a correct bill as soon as possible.
Unfortunately，two temporary secretaries you recommended to us do not speak English. We would be grateful if you could recommend two more who could speak English.

提醒某人对某事的注意：

句型
• I would like to draw your attention to（the fact that）…
• I should like to point out that…/remind you that…

续表

举例
I would like to draw your attention to the fact that we offer about 25% discount for larger orders.
I should like to point out that we guarantee that all prices are the lowest in the country.

Week 5

逐项突破（3）：PART TWO商务报告及建议书写作解析

Day 1

了解商务报告与建议书的异同

BEC 中级写作 PART TWO 的任务类型除商务信函之外，还有可能要求考生写 120～140 词的短篇商务报告或建议书（reports or proposals）。

由于这两类任务题目情景比较复杂、答题要点比较多，且需要遵从一定的框架结构，所以商务报告或建议书也是考生普遍反映比较难的一种题型。然而，这两种任务类型独成一派，是有规律可循的。

商务报告是就有关具体问题或事件做信息陈述，报告包括引言、正文和结论，形式可为备忘录或电子邮件；

建议书的格式与报告相似，但又不同于报告，建议关注的是未来，重点在于建议讨论的内容。形式也可以是备忘录或电子邮件。

任务类型	写作目的	格式	形式	语气
商务报告	提供信息 分析归纳	引言、正文和结论	备忘录或电子邮件	正式
建议书	提供信息 分析归纳 提出建议	与报告相似，但又不同于报告，建议关注的是未来，重点在于建议讨论的内容	备忘录或电子邮件	正式

一般说来，商务报告和建议书大多由下属写给上司，因而要采用正式的语言。在撰写的过程中，考生可以适当多使用一些能提高语言正式度的英语语法结构，如使用：

- 被动语态
- 复杂词汇
- 长句子
- 名词短语

- 分词短语
- 动词不定式
- 介词短语

例如下表句子的对比，考生应在写作中采用右侧的正式文体：

非正式	正式
主动语态 You must not leave the office door open during lunch hour.	被动语态 The office door should not be left open during lunch hour.
口语化用词 I think Maple Lee is the best person for this post.	复杂的商务词汇 Maple Lee is considered the most suitable person for this post.
概数 Most staff were negative about the total ban of smoking in office, although some would like to try for a while.	准确的数字 75% of staff were negative about the total ban of smoking in office, while 25% were in favor of a 2-month trial period.
短句 To make staff more satisfied and the company more efficient, a feasibility study was conducted between January and March. The study looked into whether it was possible to implement a company-wide scheme for flexible working hours.	长、复杂句 In line with recent efforts to increase staff satisfaction and company efficiency, a feasibility study was conducted between January and March to look into the possibility of implementing a company-wide flexible working hour's scheme.
动词 The problem has interrupted the normal working progress.	名词化短语 The problem has meant a severe disruption to workflow.
主观陈述 I have noticed that recently some staff members park their cars in the non-parking zones outside our office building.	客观描述 It has been noticed that recently some staff members park their cars in the non-parking zones outside our office building.

Day 2

学会分析题目

商务报告或建议书的题目中包含两种类型：

- 文字类
- 图表类（其中包括曲线图、柱状图、饼状图和表格）。

题目中有任务情景，还有一篇或多篇的正文作为提供材料，这些材料包括文字、图画或图表，这些材料上面有“手写”的注释，即考生需要完成的答题要点。

完成商务报告或建议书需要克服两个难点：

- 如何通过分析得到结论
- 如何识别并描述图表中的变化

完成商务报告和建议书需要突破的第一个难点就是要学会如何通过分析题目得出结论。下面以一道文字类题目为例，具体阐述考生应如何在写作过程中通过分析得出结论。

文字类题目与信函类题目相似，题目中给出五个内容点，考生需要准确地将五个内容点概括到报告或是建议书中。

需要注意的是，如果是建议书，考生需要使用恰当的论证方法来证明自己建议的合理性和可行性，并做到首尾呼应地提出结论。

PART TWO

- You work in the Customer Services Department of a courier firm. You have been asked to prepare a short report for your line manager about complaints.
- Look at the information below, on which you have already made some handwritten notes.
- Then, using **all** your handwritten notes, write your **report**.
- Write **120 – 140** words.

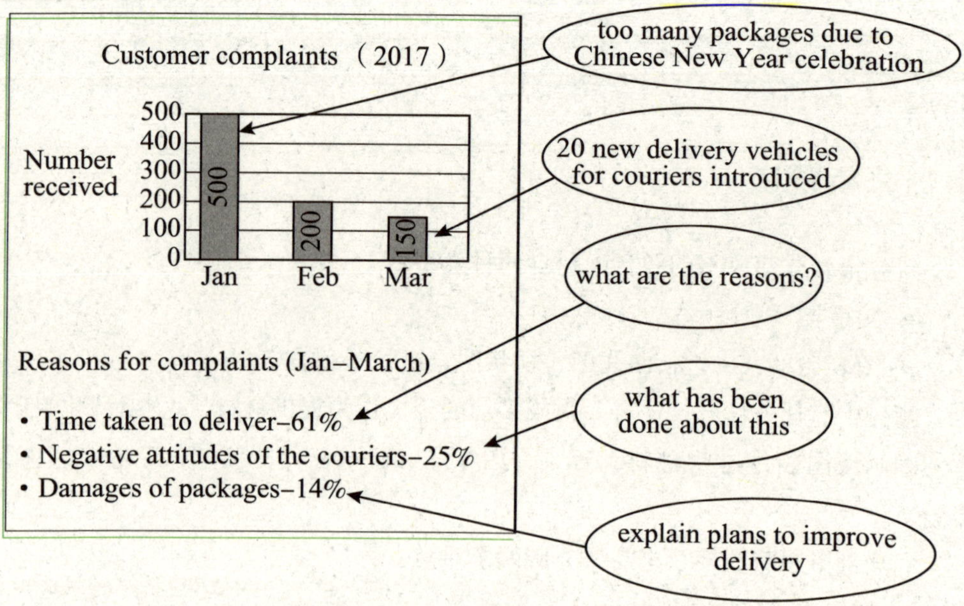

考生首先要对这五个信息点进行逐一分析：

（1）一月份客户投诉数目最高的原因：春节之前快件激增

（2）三月份采取的新措施：为快递人员配备了新的快递车

（3）需要解释投诉主要是针对送货时间的原因

（4）已经针对提高快递人员的服务态度采取了哪些措施

（5）将要采取哪些手段减少快件的破损：考生需对此提出自己的建议

通过分析我们不难看出：

- 信息点 2 是公司已经采取的新措施
- 而信息点 3、4、5 都是公司需要解决的问题
- 解决三个中的任何一个问题，考生都可以归纳到信息点 1 和 2

最重要的是：考生需要针对公司现存问题提出一到两个合理的解决办法。

Day 3

掌握写作流程

商务报告和建议书都是商务运作中不可或缺的组成部分。无论是商业报告还是建议书，考生在写作之前必须明确以下问题：

- 为什么要写这份商业报告/建议书？目的是什么？
- 读者是谁？
- 他们已知什么？
- 想要了解什么？
- 需要采取什么样的语气来写？

总的来说，考生可以遵循五步写作法：

（1）搜集必要的信息

（2）将所有信息组织、分类，找出其中逻辑顺序

（3）写草稿，将所有信息放在 Introduction，Findings，Conclusions and Recommendations的标题下

（4）检查内容是否切题

（5）更正拼写、语法和标点错误

以上一节的文字题为例，我们将通过分析 sample answer 的方式来向考生说明写商务报告或建议书需要注意的问题。

Sample Answer

Report on customer complaints

Introduction:

The purpose of this report is to summarize the reasons for customer complaints and explain plans made to improve our customer satisfaction.

Findings:

- 500 customer complaints were received in January due to the fact that we were unable to deal with the delivery pressure during the holiday season. We were pressured to deliver a great number of packages before the Chinese New Year holiday. In fact, the top reason for our customer complaints is the time taken to deliver in January.
- Apart from that, other complaints were also made concerning our couriers' attitudes and package damages. A new bonus scheme has already been introduced to improve attitudes of our couriers, rewarding those who receive positive feedback from customers.
- Finally, the introduction of 20 new delivery vehicles proved to be successful based on the fact that there was a dramatic fall of the number of customer complaints received in March.

Conclusion:

Although the cost of upgrading our delivery vehicles is quite high, the decreasing number of complaints we received proves the cost was justified.

Recommendation:

It is recommended that upgrading all our delivery vehicles might help protect packages better in transportation and shorten the delivery time, which will definitely bring benefits to the firm in the long run.

为了增强可读性考生应提供段落小标题，并注意在段与段之间空一行。在选择标题时不要为了追求报纸新闻标题那种新颖性，商务报告或建议书的标题只要准确，忠实于事实就可以了。

考生应使用名词短语而不是一个句子作标题，一般的标题都是以“report on...”开头，后面加上你要报告的内容即可。

建议书一般分为四部分（而商务报告一般包括前三项）：

- Introduction

- Findings
- Conclusion
- Recommendation

➢Introduction

在 introduction 部分，考生需指出报告的目的是什么。

可以套用以下的句型：

- The purpose/objective/aim of this report is to…
- This report aims to…

后面可以重复题目的要求，如例文中指出报告的目的就是要总结员工会议的内容。

➢Findings

在 findings 的部分，考生需要列出自己的主要发现，每条都应该是信息点的内容。为了增强可读性，考生最好在每条内容前加上项目符号或编号，并通过使用逻辑连词的方式增强文章的连贯性和整体性。

➢Conclusion

在 conclusion 部分，考生需陈述自己的结论。可以套用以下的句型：

- According to the findings above，it can be concluded that…
- Therefore，it can be concluded that…

➢Recommendation

即使在有 recommendation 这个标题的情况下，也可以直接陈述结论。需要注意的是 recommendation 以及 recommend 后面要接虚拟语气（使用动词原形）。

可以采用的句型有：

- It is recommended that…
- Based on the analysis above，we recommend that…
- It is proposed that a series of changes should be made. For instance，…

如果需要进一步展开，可以描述一下建议实施后可预期的进展或者结果。具体的说法是，建议结束之后，采用“so that…”或者“thus…”来补充说明。

Day 4

学会应对图表

完成商务报告和建议书需要突破的第二个难点就是要学会应对图表，下面就常见的图表进行举例说明。

1. 识图

为了描述图表中的变化，考生需要先学会读图表。如下图所示，图形描述通常分为三种：

- 柱状图（bar chart）
- 曲线图（graph）
- 饼状图（pie chart）

bar chart

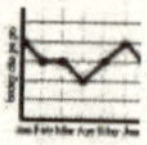
graph

pie chart

2. 柱状图

柱状图的特点是常以簇形图的形式出现，几个条形图挨在一起，组成一组，有的是多个组组成，也有的是单个的一组，还有的柱状图是分散并列的，即条形图不挨在一起。无论他们以何种形式出现，都表现出鲜明的对比。

对柱形图的描写通常以**对比**为核心。

描述柱状图常用的句型有：

- The investment **doubled/tripled** in June **compared with that** in March.
- The cell phone sales in Asia in 2016 were 1 billion **in contrast to** 300 million in Europe.
- The Chinese car dealers sold **5 times as many cars as** the American counterparts.

3. 曲线图

对于曲线图的分析，重要的是要理清曲线所显示的发展趋势，按照不同的曲线特征划分出发展阶段，对照图表的横轴查对不同的趋势发生在哪个时间段内。

以下面的曲线图：FFFC 公司 2015 财年销售额为例，考生应注意模仿对变化以及变化的程度和速度的描写所采用的手法。

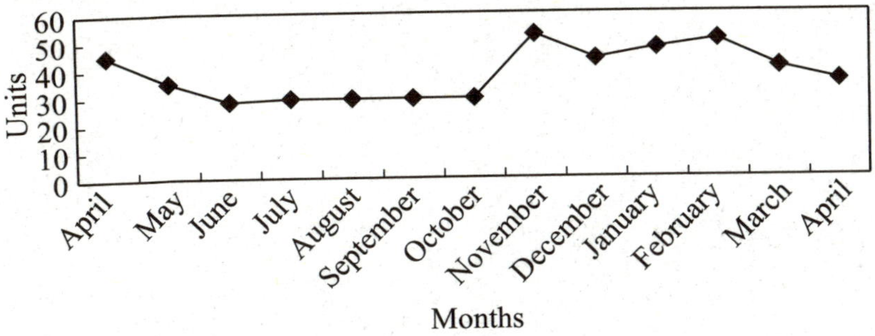

The Frosty Frozen Food Company（FFFC）has just presented its annual report. Here is a part of it:

As can be seen on this graph, the sales of Frosty Fish Fingers **fluctuated from** the start of the 2015 financial year. The year started with **a steady decline** in sales and **stabilized** in September. Sales then **rose dramatically** to a peak in November. During December sales **dipped** again, which can be attributed to the Christmas season and a general preference among the population for turkey rather than fish. However, sales **increased slowly** during January but then **declined steadily** until the end of the financial year.

4. 饼状图

饼状图是一个被分成 n 个部分的圆圈。它通常用来表示百分比。

对饼状图的描写通常以**百分比，比例**为核心。

描述饼状图常用句型有：

- Overall **87% of respondents** were at least satisfied with their holiday.

- People who prefer UK as their holiday destinations **constitute/account for** 46%.
- The two pie charts **compare the proportion of** male and female employees working in executive positions in NHG Company over a span of 5 years from Jan 2011 to Jan 2016.

Day 5

攻克写作难点

完成商务报告和建议书需要突破的难点就是要准确地将题目中给出的五个内容点概括到自己的报告和建议书中。记住，这五点就是采分点，一定要面面俱到，逐一击破。考生可以用以下 checklist 来检测自己是否出色地完成了写作任务。

Checklist for Report/Proposal Writing

（1）报告（或建议书）的名称和各小标题清楚合理

（2）五个信息点全部涵盖（可以有所侧重，但必须五点都有提及）

（3）行文流畅（是否有语法错误，是否使用了合理的 cohesive devices）

（4）总结（或建议）能做到有理有据

其中前三点是最基本的要求，而能否得到高分就要看考生是否做到了第四点。下面再举一个文字题的例子。

PART TWO

- The staff at your company were recently asked what they thought about working conditions. Your line manager has asked you to write a report summarizing their opinions and suggesting possible improvements.
- Look at the information below, on which you have already made some handwritten notes.
- Then, using all your handwritten notes, write your report.
- Write 120 – 140 words.

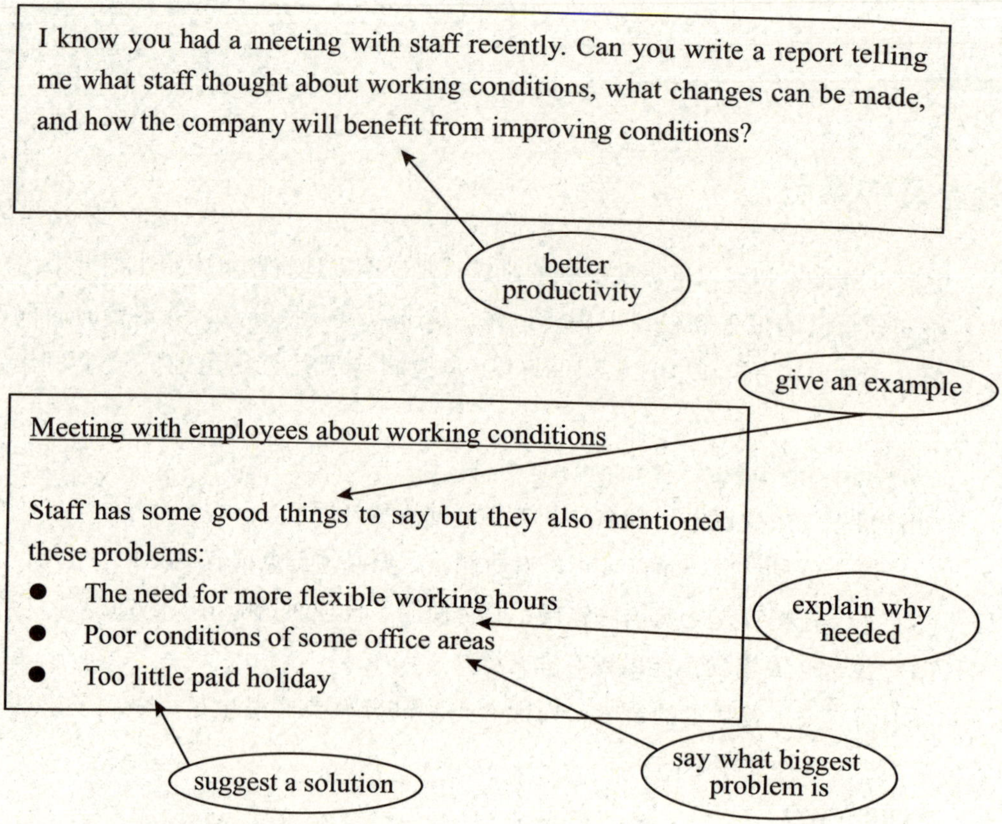

考生首先要对这五个信息点进行逐一分析：

（1）对公司的好处：提高工作效率

（2）员工对公司积极的评价：考生需举例说明

（3）需要机动灵活的工作时间的原因

（4）办公环境差的最大问题

（5）员工反映带薪假期太少：考生需对此提出自己的建议

通过分析我们不难看出：

- 信息点 2 是公司的长处或是已经得到大家认可的地方
- 而信息点 3、4、5 都是公司现在存在的问题
- 解决三个中的任何一个问题，考生都可以归纳到信息点 1
- 解决问题对公司的好处是可以提高工作效率，这样也可以保证结论言之有据

Sample answer

Report on staff opinions about working conditions

Introduction:

This report aims to summarize the results of the last staff meeting.

Findings:

- Most of the employees are quite satisfied with the new non-smoking policy, which has substantially improved the working conditions.
- However, some complained about the inflexible working hours, as they have to leave work early to fetch their children from the daycare center.
- Apart from that, the new batch of interns working here has made some office areas too crowded to ensure a quiet and uninterrupted working environment.
- Finally, the problem of too little paid holiday was also put forward by staff. I would suggest rewarding staff with chances of paid holiday to increase productivity at our workplace.

Conclusion:

In my opinion, it is vital for our staff to regularly take some time off to refresh themselves to work better.

Recommendation:

It is suggested that providing more chances of paid holiday lead to better productivity and bring benefits to the company in the long run.

虽然考试考的是商务英语的写作，但是英语写作的通用规则一样适用，比如在 Findings 标题下的四个小点分别采用了表示转折关系（However）和列点关系（apart from that；finally）的关系连词，这样一来，这部分读起来条理清晰，论证有力。

Day 6

熟记常用词汇和句型

图表的描述一般都是有规律可循的，考生需要熟练背诵一些常见的词汇和句型：

1. 表示变化的动词

当描述曲线图中变化时，我们可以使用动词来表述向上，向下和水平方向的变化。

练习：将下面的图片与相应的动词栏对应起来。

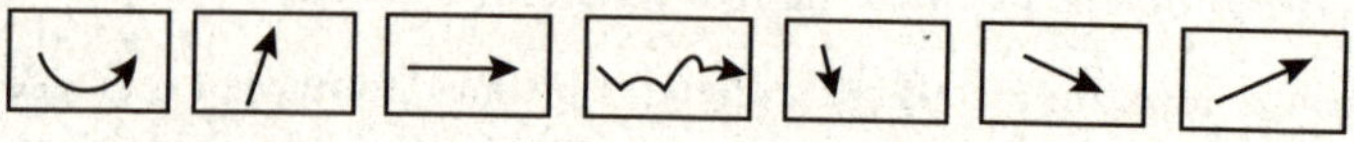

decline decrease drop fall slide	climb rise increase	soar rocket climb rise increase	crash collapse plummet plunge	flatten out hold steady level off stabilize	bounce back rally recover	fluctuate

答案：

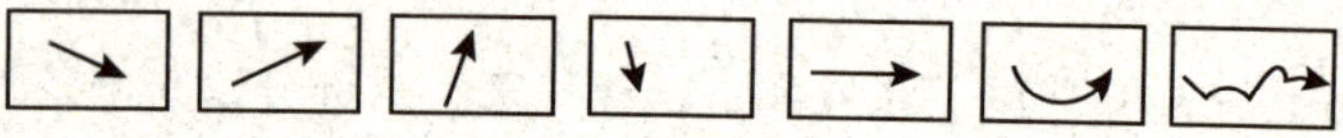

2. 动词与名词互换

大多数动词都有其相应的名词形式。通常来讲，它们是可以互换的，比如：

- to climb—a climb
- to fall—a fall

当然，也有以下特殊的情况：

- to flatten out—a flattening out
- to stabilize—a stabilization
- to level off—a leveling off
- to fluctuate—a fluctuation
- to recover—a recovery
- to hold steady—a steady hold

对于这些特殊的情况，我们在描述中通常采用动词的形式。

3. 表示变化的程度和速度的词汇

有时我们还需要对于图表的走势（trend）给予更多的细节信息，通常是表示变化的程度（degree）和变化的速度（speed of change），比如：

- The year started with a steady decline in sales and stabilized in September.
- Sales increased slowly during January and then declined steadily until the end of the financial year.

此时，考生需要使用相应的形容词或副词来对这些变化进行细节化的描写：

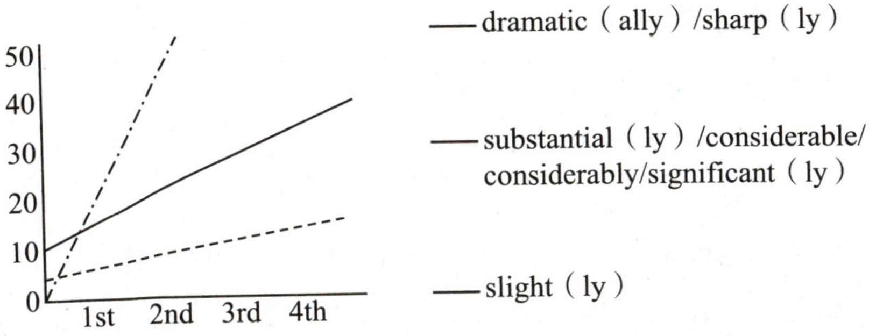

同理，描述变化的速度时也可以采用形容词或副词的形式：

- 速度快：rapid（ly）/quick（ly）/swift（ly）
- 逐步的变化：gradual（ly）/steady（ily）
- 速度慢：slow（ly）

撰写商务报告和建议书时可以使用以下句型：

1）描写写作目的

- The purpose of this report is to…investigate，evaluate，study…
- The objective of this report is to…recommend，analyze，give…
- The aim of this report is to…feedback，estimate，assess…

2）阐述结果

- It was found that…
- It was discovered that…
- There were…
- It was felt that…
- It was generally the case that…
- Most people thought that…
- Many members of staff suggested that…
- A number of people mentioned that…
- Several changes were put forward.
- Several staff members expressed the view that…
- It was proposed that…

3）提供数据

The number of imported cars	increased/jumped/rose decreased/dropped/fell fluctuated remained steady/stable stayed the same	suddenly/rapidly/dra-matically/ greatly/significantly/ sharply/steeply steadily/gradually/slowly slightly	from…to…

续表

There was a (very)	sudden/rapid/dramatic/ significant/sharp/steep steady/gradual/slow/ slight	increase/jump/rise decrease/drop/fall fluctuation	in the number of cars from…to…
The monthly profit/figures	peaked reached a peal/a high (point) bottomed out reached (the) rock-bottom		in May at 10%.
Sales	witnessed a great rise/increase/drop/fall		from…to…

4）比较和对比两种选择

- Both X and Y have…
- X is similar to Y in that there is…
- Just as in X, in Y there is…etc.
- Although Product A is faster than Product B, it is not quite as flexible.
- Despite the fact that A is more expensive than B, it is worth the extra cost.
- Even though A is not quite as popular as B, A is almost as powerful as B.

5）预测建议会产生的影响

This The policy The change	will/would/ should/ may/might	result in mean lead to allow for	a long-term improvement in productivity. a greater level of customer satisfaction. a period of low revenue in the short term. a shortage of trained staff.

Day 7

写好建议书中的建议

考生们畏惧建议书写作最主要的原因是：考生不知道如何提出可行的建议。由于考生大多数是没有任何工作经验的在校生，他们对建议往往是无从下手。其实，问题百般变化，提出的建议往往都可以归结为以下四类：

1. 建议提供培训课程、参加工作坊的机会等

这类建议主要适用于员工（包括管理人员）出现业务上的难题，需要提高自己的业务水平。这时考生可以建议 training programs/courses，workshops 等等。比如：

问题——如何提高员工和外国客户的沟通能力

Problem：We need to improve our staff's ability to communicate with foreign customers.

Suggestion：We should provide more language training opportunities for front-line staff.

问题——公司收到了对于员工服务态度的投诉

Problem：The company has received an increasing number of complaints regarding our staff attitudes.

Suggestion：A change of staff attitude is recommended. A more professional attitude will need to be encouraged through training.

2. 建议关注员工身心健康和他们的职业发展等

这类建议主要适用于员工对自己的工作现状出现了不满情绪、工作没有积极性、公司员工流失率升高等情况。这时考生可以建议公司改善员工福利待遇、提供帮助员工克服工作消极情绪的疏导手段等等。比如：

问题——如何帮助员工缓解工作压力

Problem：The feedback from our employees shows that many are stressed out and they feel they are not good at coping with stress.

Suggestion：We should offer various stress reduction programs to help employees manage stress because stress is prevalent in the workplace.

问题——员工因不满自己的职业轨迹而纷纷跳槽

Problem：The company is losing staff to its competitors because many staff are unhappy about their career paths.

Suggestion：A system of staff development should be introduced.

3. 建议公司如何降低成本、提高利润等

这类建议是最常见的考试类型——因为任何公司的运营最后归根结底都是为经济利益服务的，所以这类问题的表现形式也非常多样。最常见的包括：如何减少某一项目的花销；如何增加产品的销售进而提高利润；如何推广新产品；如何进入新的市场等等。比如：

问题——公司外聘咨询师的费用太高

Problem：The cost of employing an external consultant is unacceptably high.

Suggestion：It is suggested internal staff can be trained in the field to reduce the cost.

问题——公司的现供应商供货成本高

Problem：The company you work for is having problems with Sorenson，one of its suppliers.

Suggestion：Sorenson's costs are no longer at an advantage compared with other suppliers，therefore，it is suggested that we terminate our contract with this supplier.

4. 就某一具体问题提出更加具体的建议

这类建议往往本身已经暗示了解决方法，考生需要举出一到两个具体的做法。也就是说如果问题是需要改善办公环境，那么考生就要具体指出一到两个具体的改

善办公环境的做法，例如：实行办公室禁烟（ban smoking in offices）；购置新的办公用品/设备等（purchase new office supplies）；增加清扫人员的数目（recruit new cleaning staff）。这类题目可以千变万化，考生只需选择比较通用的建议来回答就可以了，千万不要为了单纯追求建议的新意。别忘了，只要说清楚的建议就是好建议。

问题——如何让顾客购物时更多地了解产品信息

Problem：The retail company you work for is considering how to give customers information on products and services while they shop.

Suggestion：We can install a TV system and use in-store TVs to provide customers with information of our products and services.

问题——如何推广在公司小范围内试行成功的沟通活动

Problem：The new communication activities organized in a small scale were very successful.

Suggestion：More Group-wide communication activities should be arranged for front-line and support staff.

Week 6

实战演练：模拟题

Day 1

Model Test 1

PART ONE

You are the HR manager of a company. Your assistant sent you an email and asked for 3 days off to attend a seminar on team building.

- Write a reply to her:
  - saying she cannot go
  - explaining the reason
- **Write 40 – 50 words.**

To...	Lucy Huddleston
CC...	
Subject:	Team Building Seminar

PART TWO

- You are the owner of a school supply factory. Aretailer has sent you a letter summarizing a recent negotiation. You have made some handwritten notes on the letter.

- Then, using all your handwritten notes, write a **reply** to the retailer.
- **Write 120 – 140 words.**

Dear Stewart,

It was good to see you again last week and we are delighted to inform you that Super Backpack will be included in our autumn catalogue. *(Great!)*

As promised, listed below are the points agreed upon at the meeting.

- The contract is about the Super Backpack in three colors. *(What colors?)*
- You will grant us exclusive import rights for Super Backpack in China.
- The quantity will be 10,000 pieces, with a further option of 2,000. *(3,000)*
- The price per piece will be $15.00 for the first 10,000. You will confirm the price for optional 2,000 pieces. *(Already confirmed $14.50)*
- The initial payment will be made after receiving the first batch of goods. *(before)*

Please let me know if further clarification is needed. I am looking forward to your written confirmation.

Best regards,

Jim Young
Chief Purchaser

Sample Answers

PART ONE

To…	Lucy Huddleston
CC…	
Subject:	Team Building Seminar

续表

I'm afraid you cannot attend this seminar because the annual meeting will be held next week and we have a lot of preparation to do. Also you are expected to speak at the meeting on behalf of our department. Julie

PART TWO

Dear Stewart,

Thank you for your letter concerning Super Backpack purchase. We are delighted that Super Backpack will be sold in your stores.

However, there are some small points needing clarification.

- Super Backpack is available in seven colors. Please look at the samples and confirm the three colors you have chosen.
- You mentioned in the letter the further option of 2, 000 pieces. I thought we agreed on 3, 000. Please reconfirm the quantity.
- I can now confirm the optional pieces will cost $ 14. 50 each.
- I thought we agreed on the first payment being made before the initial delivery, not after.

Please feel free to contact me if further information is needed. I look forward to hearing from you.

Yours,

Jim Young

Day 2

Model Test 2

PART ONE

- You are the training manager for a minivan manufacturer, which is going to set up a joint venture with a Brazilian automaker. You have been asked to organize a seminar on cross-cultural communication for some of the staff.
- Write a memo to all staff:
  - explaining why the training is necessary
  - saying where the seminar will be held
  - announcing which members of staff are required to attend
- **Write 40 – 50 words.**

MEMO

To:

From:

Date:

Subject:

PART TWO

- You work for a manufacturing company called SKD Ltd. The Human Resources manager has asked you to write a proposal on how the company can improve the situation of its female employees.
- Look at the information below, on which you have already made some handwritten notes.
- Then, using **all** your handwritten notes, write your **proposal**.
- **Write 120 – 140 words.**

Number of Females in Different Departments

	Current Number	Standard Number
Finance	20	21
Human Resources	5	6
Production	58	80
Sales	20	36

more female staff needed

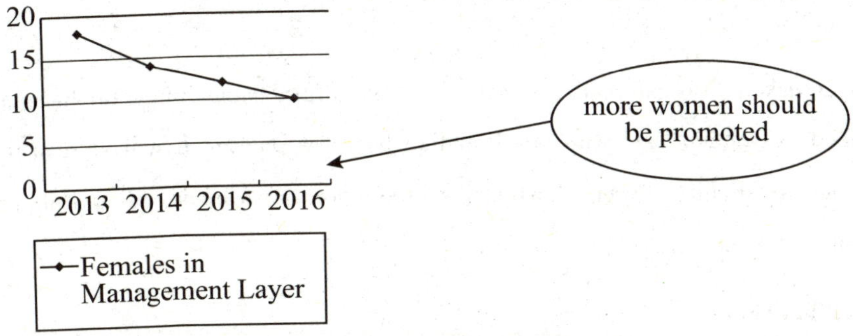

Number of Females in Management Layer

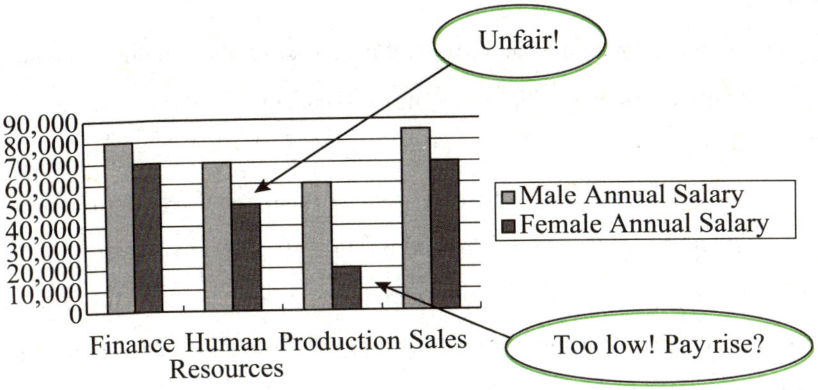

Comparison of Male and Female Salaries

Sample Answers

PART ONE

MEMO

To: All staff

From: Training Manager

Date: August 10, 2017

Subject: Seminar on Cross-Cultural Communication

I've been asked to organize a seminar on cross-cultural communication because we will need to communicate with our Brazilian business partner. It will start at 9 am, 15th August. All staff, except those of the production department, should attend the seminar.

PART TWO

Proposal on Improving the Situation of Female Employees

Introduction

This proposal aims to recommend the possible measures that could be taken to improve the situation of female employees in our company.

Findings

The table and graph clearly show that the current numbers of females in the four departments are lower than what the standard requires, especially in sales and production, where additional 16 and 22 females are needed to meet the requirements. And the number of female managers has continued to fall since 2013. Female directors decreased by about 40% in 3 years. Also women have received lower salaries than men.

Recommendations

It is recommended that more females should be recruited to balance the numbers of the two sexes. Also more women should be considered for promotion. Excellent women should be given the chance to compete with their male counterparts. And the female employees should be offered a pay rise.

Day 3

Model Test 3

PART ONE

You are the manager of the Customer Services Department. You are planning to introduce a new computer system in your department.

Write an email to all staff in your department:

- telling them when the new system will be introduced
- explaining what the advantages of the new system will be
- advising them who to contact if they have any questions

Write 40 – 50 words.

PART TWO

- Your company has agreed to pay for you to go on a training course. You have received a leaflet about a suitable course.
- Read the leaflet below, on which you have already made some handwritten notes.
- Then, using all your handwritten notes, write a proposal for your Training Manager, explaining why you would like to attend the course.
- Write 120 – 140 words.

Management: the basics

Programme includes:
- Setting targets
- Finance for beginners
- Communication skills

Very useful for me—explain why

Five-day course

Good—can learn from their experience

All trainers have at least ten years' management experience

May betters —say why

12-16 May or 1-6 September

Suggest colleague who might benefit

10% reduction if you book two or more places!

5% reduction on bookings received this month.

Great! Book now

Sample Answers

PART ONE

Dear all,

I am writing to inform you that a new computer system will be introduced as from June 13th. It will enable all staff to access on-line courses available on your internet. For any questions, please contact Mrs. Brown, EDP Department.

Suzanna

PART TWO

To: Nils Andreasen, Training Manager

From: Kelly Green

Subject: Training course

I am interested in attending the 'Management: the basics' training course.

<u>Benefits</u>

Following my recent promotion to assistant production manager, it would be very useful to study management systematically. The finance section would be particularly valuable, as financial issues are central to decisions about production.

The trainers are all experienced managers, so I'll be able to learn about management practice as well as theory.

<u>Dates</u>

Since our new product conference is in the first week of September, I would only be able to attend the May course.

<u>Additional place</u>

Juan Lopez would like to attend the course too, as he also lacks managerial experience. There is a discount if two places are booked.

<u>Booking</u>

If you agree, please book by the end of this month, in order to make a 5% saving.

Day 4

Model Test 4

PART ONE

You are a manager in an international company. You want to reduce the company's spending on courier services.

Write a memo to the staff in your department.

- explaining that spending on courier services has risen
- suggesting how savings could be made
- saying how the money saved will be used

Write 40 – 50 words.

PART TWO

- You work for a market research company. One of your clients—a travel agent—has asked you to advise them on e-commerce. Look at the figures they supplied below on which you have already made some comments. Then, using all these comments, write your report.
- Write 120 – 140 words.

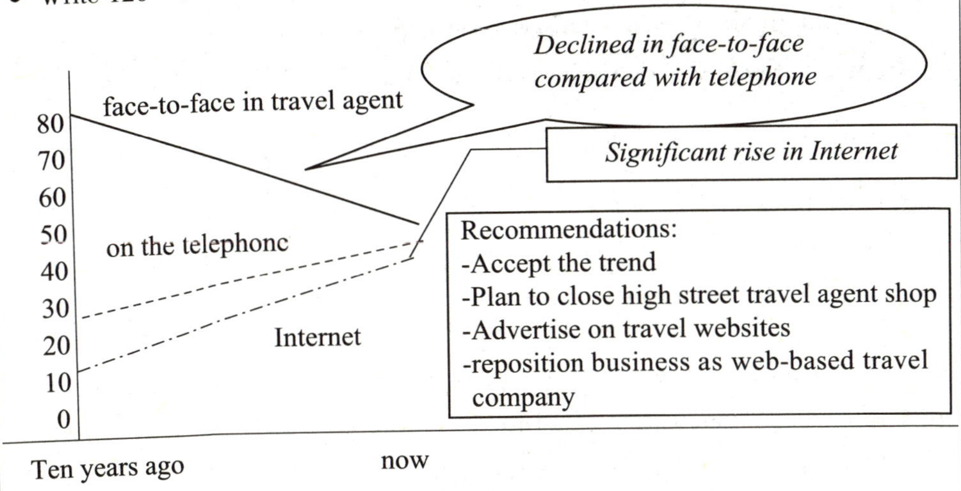

Sample Answers

PART ONE

<u>Memo</u>

To: All

From: Lucy Smith

Subject: Reducing spending on courier services

The company's spending on courier services has risen by 15% in the last year. We can reduce expenditure by sending letters and documents by email whenever possible. All the money that we save will be spent on improving our training facilities.

PART TWO

Sunrays Travel Agency-E-commerce

The purpose of this report is to evaluate the current situation of e-commerce in Sunrays Travel Agency in connection with other traditional ways of running the business.

We have investigated it using some comments and figures that the company provided, analyzing its operations form ten years ago to now.

We could see a sudden decline in face-to-face transactions from 80% to 50% approximately, due to the fact that customers have changed their attitudes and prefer other ways of operating. For example, telephone reservations have experienced an increase of 20% approximately and Internet booking has risen significantly.

As regards the market tendency, we suggest that the company should plan to close High Street shops. Meanwhile, we advise the company to change its business strategy and move gradually to a web-based travel agency.

Day 5

Model Test 5

PART ONE

You are a HR manager and you plan to invite Mindsets Company to give personnel training course on cultural diversity.

Write an email to your assistant:

- asking her/him to contact the company
- saying the number of participants and the duration of time
- suggesting available weekends

Write 40 – 50 words.

To...	Grace
CC...	
Subject:	Personnel training

PART TWO

- The staff at your company were recently asked what they thought about the company canteen. Your line manager has asked you to write a proposal summarizing their opinions and suggesting possible improvements.

- Look at the information below, on which you have already made some handwritten notes.
- Then, using all your handwritten notes, write your proposal.
- Write 120 – 140 words.

how was the information obtained

I know you had a meeting with staff recently. Can you write a proposal telling me what staff thought about the company canteen, why the number of staff using the company cantten at mealtimes has been falling? Can you also suggest some possible ways to encourage staff to use the canteen?

suggest something

elaborate on this

Meeting with employess about the company canteen

Staff mentioned these:

- Menu
- Conditions of the canteen
- Pirce too high

compared with whom?

what problem?

Sample Answers

PART ONE

Grace,

Could you please contact Mindsets to organize a personnel training course on the topic of cultural diversity? We will have ten participants and the course should last two days. I suggest the weekend of 11/12 June or, if that is not possible, the following weekend.

Thanks.

Nick

PART TWO

Proposal on the low utility rate of staff canteen

Introduction

The proposal aims to examine key reasons why our employees prefer other lunch venues as opposed to our staff canteen and suggest possible ways for improvement. Semi-formal interviews with 20 staff members were conducted to obtain the following opinions.

Findings

- **Menu.** It was pointed out by many employees that the menu failed to offer any variety. Set menus can no longer cater to people's needs for healthy and balanced diet.

- **Conditions of the canteen**. The main problem is that the canteen is too crowed at peak hour.
- **Price too high**. Compared with many other fast food restaurants within a five-minute walking distance from our premises, our food is too expensive.

Recommendations

It is strongly suggested that we should introduce flexible opening hours to avoid too many people dining at peak hour and provide cheaper, more healthy and diversified meals to attract our employees.

Day 6

Model Test 6

PART ONE

You are a HR manager. You plan to hold interviews next week.

Write an email to your PA Susan:

- telling her the post you want to interview for
- asking her to call the candidates
- reminding her to inform the other interviewers of the schedule

Write 40 – 50 words.

To…	Susan
From…	Robert
Subject:	Interviews

PART TWO

- Your line manager has decided to review the staff situation in your department. You have been asked to write a report concerning this.
- Look at the information below, on which you have already made some handwritten notes.
- Then, using all your handwritten notes, write your report.
- Write 120 – 140 words.

	Number of staff leaving the department	Number of recruitment
2001	2	2
2002	3	2
2003	6	3

what reason?

not enough

Number of new staff needed: 4
possible new recruitment methods: specialist recruiment agency local recruitment agency

say what type of staff needed

compare

say what effect this will have

To...	All Staff
CC...	
Subject:	Training opportunities
The company decides to provide overseas training opportunities to staff that have stayed at least five years with the company. Please submit your application...	

Sample Answers

PART ONE

I am going to hold interviews for the post of Marketing Manager on Friday morning next week. Please ring the 5 candidates and tell them the date and the venue of the interview. Please also remember to write memos of the agenda to the other interview committee members.

PART TWO

Report on further staff recruitment

Introduction

The purpose of this report is to assess the current staff situation in our department and recommend ways of recruiting staff.

Findings

Our department is experiencing a serious understaffing problem due to the fact that in 2003 we were only able to recruit three new staff whereas six people left our department, which was caused by, as reported by some staff, the fact that employees were unhappy about their career paths here. There is an urgent need for us to employ both administrative staff and IT personnel.

The company is promising to offer overseas training opportunities to loyal staff, which provides a great opportunity for us to attract new employees.

Local recruitment agency

The local agency is good at recruiting skilled office staff but not people with specialist IT skills.

Specialist recruitment agency

The IT recruitment agency deals with the entire application and screening process. Although their costs are high, it would enable the company to recruit more quickly.

Day 7

Model Test 7

PART ONE

You are a marketing manager and going to market a new shampoo product.

Write an email to team members:

- saying who the target customers are
- telling them the amount of budget
- suggesting a meeting to collect ideas

Write 40 – 50 words.

To…	Marketing team
CC…	
Subject:	Marketing a new shampoo

PART TWO

- Your Managing Director has asked you to reply to the letter below which is about a proposed educational visit to your company by a local school. He has written his comments on the letter.
- Write a letter of 120 – 140 words to the headteacher explaining the changes the Managing Director would like to make to the visit.
- Write on your answer sheet.
- Please do not include postal addresses.

Dear Mr. Johnson,

Thank you for your recent letter accepting our request for an educational visit to your company.

I have spoken to the students concerned as well as the teacher who will accompany them. They are a group of 40 students, aged between 18 and 19, and will be taking part in the visit as part of their career development program.

[too many—25 maximum]

I would like to suggest Friday 18th December. The group will leave here at 8:00 am and should be with you by 8:40 am.

[Monday of following week better]

I understand the training officer is willing to give a talk to the students about the company's training program. This will be of considerable value, and I wonder if it would be at the beginning of the visit.

[training officer not available until 10:30]

Finally, would it be possible for the students to talk to some new employees in an informal "question and answer" session?

[No, sorry! Cannot release employees from duties.]

I would be grateful if you could inform me as to whether these proposals are suitable and would like to thank you once again for your co-operation.

Yours sincerely,

Robert MacNeil

Headteacher

Sample Answers

PART ONE

Dear all,

We are going to launch promotional activities on a shampoo product which may attract women aged 12 – 25. We now have a fund of 5,000 dollars for marketing events. Please meet at the conference room at 9 a. m. on the following Monday to brainstorm ideas for possible activities.

PART TWO

Dear Mr. MacNeil,

Thank you for your letter, in which you put forward some suggestions for the proposed visit to our company.

There are, however, a few changes which I would like to make to your suggestions:

* Our company is not able to receive 40 students but a maximum of 25 would be acceptable.
* You suggested the date of 18th Friday. Unfortunately, a conference has been arranged on that day. Would Monday of the following week be available for you?
* The training officer will not come back until 10:30, so his talk to the students will have to be delayed.

As to your request to have our new employees talk to your students, we regret to tell you that we can not release them from their duties.

If you have any further questions, please feel free to contact me.

Yours sincerely,

David Johnson

宝典：得分工具百宝箱

1. 商务英语核心 100 名词

List of 100 Essential Business English Nouns/Phrases

account	department	insurance policy	promotion
acquisition	decrease	inventory	purchase
after-sales service	direct marketing	incentive	personal assistant
agenda	deadline	inquiry	practice
allowance	efficiency	job description	publicity
authorization	employer/ee	label	quality control
bank loan	enquiry	launch	resources
brand	environment	line manager	refund policy
budget	equipment	margin	reminder
bonus	estimate	market share	recruitment
business plan	e-commerce	motivation	retailer
capital	expansion	networking	trade fair
commission	flexibility	newsletter	risk
competitor	field	outlet	salary

续表

confirmation	function	offer	sales
cost	feedback	option	schedule
client	gap	order	signature
complaint	goods	on-the-job training	stock
consultant	guarantee	payment	staff facilities
customer satisfaction	headquarters	performance	suggestion
candidate	health & safety	permission	supply
company regulations	hourly rate	production method	support
downturn	industry	product	transport
distribution	instructions	paid leave	turnover
delivery	interest	profit	target

常用名词/短语练习：

A. 请选择适当的名词填空

confirmation	launch	industry	promotion	turnover
acquisition	recruitment	account	target	retailer
purchase	outlet	margin	distribution	networking
expansion	efficiency	recruitment	incentive	transport

(1) The company's production ________ is 1, 000 refrigerators each week.

(2) We need to acquire the services of a ________ agent as well as a business consultant in order to gain local knowledge.

(3) We enjoy a good business relationship with all the leading wholesalers and ________ in that line.

(4) According to our estimate, the maximum annual ________ will be over 200, 000 dollars.

(5) Our Beijing-based marketing branch has just won two Edinburgh ________.

(6) When can we expect your ________ of the order?

(7) We would like you to pay for your ________ now and we guarantee that the goods will get to you within three days.

(8) The meeting is important, since it's about the ________ of our new product.

(9) Some methods of advertising or ________ are more suitable to certain products or services than others.

(10) The most important next step for the company was to employ a full-time Human Resources Manager. The company has needed someone to deal with ________ policy for a long time.

(11) We are responsible for developing a new market to increase our profit ________.

(12) Our company has been in the furniture ________ for many years.

(13) ________ is not simply an information exchange between you and another person. It involves establishing relationships with people who will often become your friends and community of colleagues as you go through your career.

(14) The successful ________ of a profitable paper recycling company has helped our company to increase its revenue dramatically.

(15) To increase our market share, it is recommended that we should open two more retail ________ in this region.

(16) As a result of ________, our company has recently hired a lot of new people for all levels of the company. However, the original staff do not mix or communicate well with the new staff.

(17) We should hire an office design consultant to design our new offices because good office design can save our company money and improve ________.

(18) Because of our urgent need for new staff, we recommend that local agencies are used to recruit administrative staff and specialist IT ________ agencies for IT personnel.

(19) Your company has received a complaint about some goods which arrived damaged, but you don't know if the damage happened before they left your

company or during ________ .

(20) Some of the most common ________ used to help motivate people are recognition, money, health and help with child care.

答案：

(1) target	(2) distribution	(3) retailers	(4) turnover
(5) accounts	(6) confirmation	(7) purchase	(8) launch
(9) promotion	(10) recruitment	(11) margin	(12) industry
(13) networking	(14) acquisition	(15) outlets	(16) expansion
(17) efficiency	(18) recruitment	(19) transport	(20) incentives

B. 请选择适当的短语填空

company regulations	paid leave	business plan	quality control
on-the-job training	customer satisfaction	market share	after-sales service
refund policy	insurance policy	line manager	trade fair
production method	direct marketing	health & safety	

(1) Your ________ at head office would like a report about three of the stores in your region, including a recommendation to close one of them.

(2) We offer an attractive package of compensation including: competitive salary, performance-based bonus, medical care benefits and 2-week ______ every year.

(3) The ________ department has got some feedback on the product quality.

(4) _______ state that paid compassionate leave of absence can only be given in the case of the death of a close relative and for no longer than a maximum of ten days.

(5) In order to reach out to a greater number of potential clients, we suggest launching a ________ campaign in the New York area.

(6) Two office ________ concerns raised by our employees are inadequate lighting and unsuitable furniture.

(7) If we are to stabilize or better rebuild our ________, we could propose a drop in price and a fierce advertising campaign.

(8) To improve our ________ we are extending the service period on all our

equipment to two years.

(9) We recommend therefore that higher priority is given to ________, and that experienced sales managers spend time in the field, working with new sellers and those who are performing less well.

(10) For all ________ we recommend that a project team should be set up well in advance to handle all the arrangements.

(11) The ________ plan must not only detail who is responsible for carrying out a particular task, but it also must specify who is responsible for checking the work.

(12) It is suggested that we should choose PBK Removals because the company offers a comprehensive ________ for damages.

(13) The new ______ has given our company a critical edge over our competitors.

(14) It has come to our attention that customers are not happy with the way we deal with product returns, so it is suggested that we should revise our ________.

(15) Every company has to review their ________ annually or even quarterly, to stay ahead of the game.

答案：

(1) line manager	(2) paid leave	(3) after-sales service
(4) Company regulations	(5) direct marketing	(6) health and safety
(7) market share	(8) customer satisfaction	(9) on-the-job training
(10) trade fairs	(11) quality control	(12) insurance policy
(13) production method	(14) refund policy	(15) business plan

2. 商务英语核心 100 动词

List of 100 Essential Business English Verbs

accept	count	invoice	purchase
allow	decide	join	raise
admit	decrease	lend	reach

续表

advertise	deliver	lengthen	receive
advise	develop	lower	recruit
afford	dismiss	maintain	reduce
approve	dispatch	manage	refuse
authorize	distribute	measure	reject
avoid	divide	mention	remind
borrow	drop	obtain	remove
break	employ	order	reply
build	encourage	organize	resign
buy	establish	owe	respond
calculate	estimate	own	return
comply	exchange	pack	recommend
cancel	extend	participate	sell
change	forbid	pay	send
charge	fix	plan	separate
check	fund	present	shorten
choose	get（worse）	prevent	split
complain	improve	process	structure
complete	interfere	produce	succeed
confirm	inform	promise	suggest
consider	install	promote	write
convince	invest	provide	vary

利用常用动词写作举例：

afford　买得起，有能力作
We are able to afford superb facilities since we achieved a high level of profit last year. 由于我们去年利润率较高，我们可以买得起如此优良的设备。

续表

authorize 授权
As a franchisor we have the right to authorize the chain stores to use our trademark. 作为直营店特许人，我们可以授权连锁商店使用我们的商标。
cancel 取消
I'm awfully sorry that we have to cancel the order because of finance shortage. 我实在很抱歉由于资金短缺我们不得不取消订单。
charge 收取，索要金额
We will charge you only 80% of the regular service fees for the maintenance service after the guarantee period. 超过保证期限之后，我们只收取你们 80% 的常规维修费。
confirm 确认
Please confirm the letter of credit ASAP. 请尽快确认信用证。
convince 使相信
It is our responsibility to convince consumers that the GM foods we produce are safe. 我们公司有责任使消费者确信我们生产的转基因食品是安全的。
deliver 交货，送货
Since you promise that you will deliver the goods on time, we don't insist on the changing. 既然你们承诺会按时交货，那我们就不再坚持更改了.
dispatch 分派
Two loads of woolen cloth were dispatched to the factory on December 12th. 两车的羊毛制衣于 12 月 12 日派送至工厂。
distribute 分销
Our company aims eventually to distribute products throughout the European Union. 我们公司的最终目标是通过欧盟分销产品。

续表

extend　扩大，延伸
Our company is one of the biggest furniture suppliers in China, which has extended our services to most of the Northeast area. 我们公司是中国最大的家具供应商之一，服务已经延伸至中国东北大部分地区。
fund　提供资金
We'll need accurate costings before we can agree to fund the scheme. 我们需要准确的成本核算，然后才能同意资助这个方案。
install　安装
We have our own computer specialists and engineers that can not only build your required systems, but also install all the necessary software and networks. 我们有自己的电脑专家和工程师，所以我们不仅可以建立你们所需要的系统，而且还能安装全部的必要软件和网络。
invest　投资
In order to ensure competitiveness we will continue to invest heavily in marketing development and personnel training. 为确保我公司的竞争力，我们会继续大量投资于市场开发和员工培训。
invoice 寄发票，开票给
We'll invoice you for parts and labour. 我们会把零件和劳务费的发票寄给你们。
lengthen　延长
I suggest we should lengthen the guarantee service of our product. 我建议延长我们产品的保修年限。
maintain　维持，保持
We may take advantage of advertising to maintain our customers' brand loyalty. 我们可以利用广告保持用户的品牌忠实度。

续表

participate　参加
We're willing to participate in the bid which you advertised in China Daily. Would you please tell me the detail of the conditions? 我们想参加你们登在中国日报上的招标。您能否告知我们招标条件的细节？
present　作报告
Our marketing manager is supposed to present a report to all staff at the meeting. 市场部经理会在全体会议上作汇报。
promise　承诺，许诺
We can promise you that, if you purchase our product, you will be getting quality. 我们可以保证，如果您购买我们的产品，您一定会得到高质量的货品。
purchase　采购，购买
Since this is the first time you purchased from us, I' like to listen to your opinion about inspection. 由于这是你们第一次购买我们的商品，我很想听一听你方对检验的意见。 Please let us know what kind of equipment you would like to purchase. 请尽快告知贵公司想购进何种设备。 The item we'd like to purchase is the advanced drilling equipment. 我们主要想购进比较先进的钻探设备。
recruit　雇佣，招募
We only recruit go-getters who will be actively involved in the company's development. 我们只打算招募有经验的人员，他们应该能够积极参与公司的发展。 Our firm is hoping to recruit a new sales director. 我们公司打算聘请一名销售主管。 The sales department will be recruiting extra staff for the Christmas period. 销售部门将在圣诞节期间额外雇佣一些员工。
split　分割
That still leaves a gap of 20 dollars as to the price. We suggest we split the difference so that we can both be satisfied. 关于产品价格还有 20 美元的差额。我方建议各自分担一半差额，这样双方都能满意这个价格。

常用动词练习：

COMPANY SMOKING POLICY

(1) Employees are ______ to smoke anywhere except in the designated areas. It is possible that anyone who consistently ______ this rule will lose his/her job.

(2) Smokers are ________ to use rooms 4B and 6C for cigarette breaks or coffee breaks. They are permitted to take up to four five-minute breaks a day to smoke, excluding lunch and coffee breaks. They are not obliged to tell their supervisors when they go for an ________ cigarette break but are not allowed to take more than four breaks without special permission.

(3) Smokers are strictly forbidden to empty ashtrays into wastepaper bins as there is a possibility that this will cause a fire. You are ________ not to leave the doors of the smoking rooms open, as this ________ with the ventilation system.

(4) Clients and visitors to the company are also obliged to ________ with the smoking regulations. To avoid causing embarrassment to visitors, it is ________ that you explain our policy to them on arrival and ask if they are smokers. If so, use the special meeting room provided for smokers; for small, informal discussions it is also possible for you to use the smoking section of the reception hall.

答案：

(1) forbidden	breaks	(2) allowed	approved
(3) advised	interferes	(4) comply	recommended

3. 商务英语核心 60 形容词

商务英语信函、报告和建议书中的形容词很特殊，因为要求正式文体，所以形容词必须是不带感情色彩的中性形容词，这与新闻英语中的形容词正好相反。形容词一般是客观描述性的形容词。

absent	economical	internal	positive
acceptable	economic	intensive	profitable
accurate	electronic	increasing	prompt
additional	essential	innovative	punctual
administrative	extra	leading	redundant
annual	effective	mass	relevant
aware	executive	minor	satisfactory
available	final	necessary	sufficient
brief	former	negative	time-consuming
competitive	formal	negotiable	temporary
creative	frequent	original	typical
current	flexible	pleasant	urgent
convenient	global	popular	unacceptable
door-to-door	gradual	portable	valuable
dramatic	independent	productive	well-qualified

用适当的形容词填空。

(1) As a result of expansion, our company now urgently needs to hire five new general office staff and three ________ electronic engineers.

(2) We can make our company more attractive to potential employees by offering things such as ________ hours and work at home options.

(3) The factory intends to make 200 workers ________.

(4) Your supervisor requested you to write to your cruise customers to ask them if the new dates are ________.

(5) The ________ turnover of our company is $ 1 million.

(6) The worst problem is that we are struggling to find enough ________ staff to fill Christmas orders.

(7) It is too ________ to recruit junior personnel ourselves, so we should try to

use recruitment agencies in the future.

(8) Using ________ trainers reduces the cost per head for training. It also allows our company to offer training which really meets the needs of our employees.

(9) Working with ________ trainers not only brings new ideas into the company, but also allows the company to train more staff more quickly.

(10) This method is ________ because you can insert an advertisement at short notice and your ad can contain details, such as prices and telephone numbers or special offer coupons giving discounts.

答案：

(1) well-qualified (2) flexible (3) redundant (4) acceptable
(5) annual (6) temporary (7) time-consuming (8) internal
(9) external (10) convenient

4. BEC 中级写作常用短语

a shortage of cash	现金短缺
advertising campaign	广告宣传活动
advertising executive	广告主管人员
annual leave	年假
annual report	年度报告
answering machine	录音电话
articles on display	展台商品
ASAP	尽快
current assets	流动资产
attach importance to team building	重视团队建设
balance sheet	资产负债表、平衡表
base pay	基本工资
behind schedule	进度落后于计划

续表

benefit premium	福利津贴
benefit system	福利制度
benefits package	一揽子福利计划（工资之外的福利，如健康保险，住房或股票等）
bonus points	（消费）积分
brand leader	畅销品牌
brand loyalty	顾客对品牌的忠诚
business objectives	商务目标
business trip	商务旅行
cancel an order	取消订单
capital investment	资本投资
cash flow gap	现金流量差额
cash flow	现金流
cash on delivery	货到付款
cash surplus	现金盈余
catalogue price	商品目录价格
chief accountant	首席会计
company culture/enterprises culture	公司文化
company image	公司形象
company performance	公司绩效
company values	公司价值观
consumer confidence	消费者信心
confirm an order	确认订单
consistent quality	稳定的质量
corporate business area（business district，commercial district，commercial area）	商务区、商务地段

续表

corporate hospitality	商务接待
cost-cutting measures	降低成本的措施
customer-focused	以顾客为中心的
deadline for registration	报名截止日期
dealership network	经销商网络
delivery costs	交货费用，运费
delivery time	交货时间
department training budget	部门培训预算
develop team work	开拓团队协作
distribution network	物流网络，配送网络
effective management style	有效的管理方式
emphasize team spirit	强调团队精神
expenses claim	报销申报
expenses claims sheet	报销单
final payment	最后付款
financing costs	筹措成本，融资成本
follow-up evaluation	后续评估
food and accommodation	食宿
franchise to build and operate the tunnel	建造和经营隧道的特许经权
free delivery area	免费送货区
go for profit	追求利润
half-year sales report	半年度销售报告
Head Office	总部
hotel bills	旅馆住宿费
industrial estate（trading estate，industrial park）	工业园区

续表

information packs	资料袋
inventory control/management	库存控制/管理
leasehold property (opp. Freehold property)	租赁财产（反义：终身保有的财产）
line manager	直属经理，业务经理
local adaptation	产品的本土化
logistics service	物流服务
loyalty scheme	忠实（顾客）奖励计划
mail order company	邮购公司
major brands	主导品牌
make delivery	发货
management consultant	管理顾问
managerial skills	管理技能
(a net profit) margin of 30%	30%的纯利润率
Marketing and Sales Directors	营销和销售主管
marketing industry	营销行业
marketing mix	营销组合
marketing strategy	营销策略
operational margins	经营利润
overhead	企业一般管理费用，日常开支
PA (personal assistant)	助理
pension scheme	养老金计划
performance evaluation	绩效评估
place an order	发出订单
point-of-sale	销售网点
potential profits	潜在利润

续表

premises	（企业、机构等使用的）经营场地、生产场地、办公场所
pre-tax profits	税前利润
price-cutting	降价，价格战
pro-business environment	对商务有利的环境
product life cycle	产品寿命周期
production facilities	生产设备
(customer) profile	（顾客）档案
public transportation fares	公交车费
R & D project	研发项目
retail food market	食品零售市场
running costs	管理费用，经营成本
sales department	销售部门
sales staff	销售人员
sales volume	销售额
set objectives	确立目标
settle the balance	结清余额
set-up costs	创办成本
small profit and quick returns	薄利多销
staff complaints	员工投诉
staff turnover	人员流动率
stick to the schedule	严格按计划进行
supplier management	供货商管理
take delivery	取货
target customer	销售对象，目标客户
target market	目标市场

续表

team building	团队建设
time schedule	时间安排表
trade fair	贸易洽谈会
trading volume	贸易额，交易额
traveling expenses	旅行费用
(annual) turnover	(年) 营业额
vendor quotation	厂家报价
voice mail	语音信息
work extra time	加班

5. 常见公司部门和职位

Departments of a company

accounting department/accounts department	会计处
customer service/service team	客户服务部
EDP team (EDP = electronic data processing)	电子数据处理小组
engineering department	工程部
export department/export team/export sales department	外销部，出口部
import department/import team	进口部
IT department (IT = information technology)	信息技术部
logistics department	物流部
manufacturing department/production department	生产科
marketing department	市场营销部
materials administration	物资管理部
personnel department/staff department/human resources	人事部，人力资源部

续表

public relations team/public relations department	公关部
purchasing department	采购部，（物资）供应科
research and development team	研发部门
sales department	销售部
Secretary's office	秘书处
shipping department/dispatch department	运输部，送货部
technical support team	技术支援小组
warehousing department	仓储部

Jobs

analyst	分析师
assistant（e. g. purchasing assistant）	助理
buyer	采买员
CEO（Chief Executive Officer）	首席执行官
co-director	副总监
commercial agent	商务代表
director general	主任
director of boards	董事长
economist	经济师
export sales manager	外销部经理
management board	管理委员会
managing director	总经理
purchasing manager	采购部经理
sales manager	销售部经理

续表

sales representative	销售代表
senior executive	高级行政官
service engineer	维护工程师
treasurer，CFO（Chief Financial Officer）	财务主管
warehouse manager	仓储部经理
wholesale distributing manager	批发部经理

6. BEC 中级写作题目中常见“手写标注”及应答句式

Asking for information on this.

- Could you also let me know…
- I'd be grateful if you could tell me…

Compare these statistics.

- In 2007，the sales were 25% lower than this year.
- While in 2005 we sold…，this year we have managed to sell…

Complain about this.

Another thing which went wrong was…

Suggest that they do this.

- It might be a good idea to…
- You could also consider contacting…

Remind him to do this.

Please remember to…

Summarise these statistics.

Basically, these figures show that...

Explain why this happened.

- The reason why this occurred is that...
- This happened because...

Apologise about this.

I'm sorry to say that...

Recommend that this is done.

I would strongly recommend that...

Say that this is a possibility.

However, it might be possible to...

7. 常用商务小话题介绍

了解常用商务话题，对 BEC 中级写作有以下好处：

- 准确理解考题情景
- 准确理解考点要求
- 准确描述公司业务
- 合理扩充答题内容
- 恰当提供解决办法

➢After-sales service（售后服务）

Customer support following the purchase of a product or service. In some cases, after-sales service can be almost as important as the initial purchase. The manufacturer, retailer, or service provider determined what is included in any warranty (or guarantee) package. This will include the duration of the warranty, maintenance and/or replacement policy, items included/excluded, labor costs, and speed of response.

➢Annual leave（年假）

An employee may use annual leave for vacations, rest and relaxation, and personal business or emergencies. An employee has a right to take annual leave, subject to the right of the supervisor to schedule the time at which annual leave may be taken.

➢Business decisions（业务决策）

One of the greatest skills a leader can have is the ability to make effective business decisions. Business leaders make dozens of decisions every day that influence the success of the company while also having an impact on employees, customers or the marketplace. Developing such a skill requires a combination of education, experience and intuition.

➢Business hours（营业/上班时间）

Business hours are the hours during the day in which business is commonly conducted. Typical business hours vary widely by country. By observing common informal standards for business hours, workers may communicate with each other more easily and find a convenient divide between work life and home life.

➢Chain store（连锁店）

Two or more shops or outlets that have the same owner and sell similar lines of merchandise. For example, the brand name, 7-Eleven is now part of an international chain of convenience stores. It is the largest chain store with more than 36, 842 outlets operating around the world.

➢Company newsletter（公司简讯）

A newsletter is one way to share information with employees, customers and vendors. A company newsletter usually includes the following sections: A "guest" section which shares the human side of the business by inviting employees, management, and vendors to contribute columns; A "Tip" section which gives suggestions on how to improve productivity, such as how to use email effectively and how to conduct meetings; A "in-depth look" section which examines different operating areas to foster teamwork and help employees understand how their work contributes to the company's success; A "training" section that supports the company's values, such as ethics, diversity and innovation. An internal company newsletter can be an important tool to keep employees in the loop about company activities, policies, products, and services.

➢Convenience store（便利店）

A convenience store is a small store or shop that sells items such as candy, ice-cream, soft drinks, lottery tickets, cigarettes and other tobacco products, newspapers and magazines, along with a selection of processed food and perhaps some groceries. Stores that are part of gas stations may also sell motor oil, windshield washer fluid, and maps.

➢Coupon（代金券）

In marketing a coupon is a ticket or document that can be exchanged for a financial discount or rebate when purchasing a product. Customarily, coupons are issued by manufacturers of consumer packaged goods or by retailers, to be used in retail stores as a part of sales promotions. They are often widely distributed through mail, magazines, newspapers, the Internet, and mobile devices such as cell phones.

➢Department store（百货商店）

A department store is a retail establishment which specializes in satisfying a wide range of the consumer's personal and residential durable goods product needs; and at the same time offering the consumer a choice multiple merchandise lines, at variable price points, in all product categories. Department stores usually sell products including apparel, furniture, home appliances, electronics, and additionally select other lines of products such as paint, hardware, toiletries, cosmetics, photographic equipment, jewelry, toys and sporting goods.

➢Employee turnover（人员流动）

Employee turnover is a ratio comparison of the number of employees a company must replace in a given time period to the average number of total employees. Simple ways to describe it are "how long employees tend to stay" or "the rate of traffic through the revolving door." High turnover can be harmful to a company's productivity if skilled workers are often leaving and the worker population contains a high percentage of novice workers.

➢Warranty（保单）

In commercial and consumer transactions, a warranty is a collateral assurance that certain facets of an article or service sold is as factually stated or legally implied by the seller, and that often provides for a specific remedy such as repair or replacement in the event the article or service fails to meet the warranty. For example, the machine is still under warranty.

➢Inventory turnover（存货周转率）

The ratio of a company's annual sales to its inventory; or equivalently, the fraction of a year that an average item remains in inventory. Low turnover is a sign of inefficiency, since inventory usually has a rate of return of zero. For instance, if a company was able to generate $10 million in sales but averaged $5 million in inventory, the inventory turnover would be 10 million/5 million = 2. This number indicates that there would be 2 inventory turns per year, meaning that it would take 6 months to sell the entire inventory.

➢Joint venture（合资企业）

A joint venture is an entity formed between two or more parties to undertake economic activity together. The parties agree to create a new entity by both contributing equity, and they then share in the revenues, expenses, and control of the enterprise.

➢Market research（市场调查）

Market research is any organized effort to gather information about target markets or customers. It is a very important component of business strategy. Market research is one of the key factors used in maintaining competitiveness over competitors. Market research provides important information to identify and analyze the market need, market size and competition. Market-research techniques encompass both qualitative techniques such as focus groups, in-depth interviews, and ethnography, as well as quantitative techniques such as customer surveys, and analysis of secondary data.

➢Maternity leave（产假）

A period of time that the mother of a new baby is allowed away from work. Parental leave is an employee benefit that provides paid or unpaid time off work to care for a child or make arrangements for the child's welfare. Often, the term parental leave includes maternity, paternity, and adoption leave.

➢Natural wastage（人员流失）

A reduction in the number of people employed by an organization, which happens when people leave their jobs and the jobs are not given to anyone else.

➢Profit margin（利润率）

Profit margin, net margin, net profit margin or net profit ration all refer to a measure of profitability. It is calculated by finding the net profit as a percentage of the revenue. Profit margin is an indicator of a company's pricing policies and its ability to control costs.

➢Retail（零售）

To sell in small quantities, as in a shop, directly to the consumers.

➢Revenue（收入）

For a company, this is the total amount of money received by the company for goods sold or services provided during a certain time period. It also includes all net sales, exchange of assets; interest and any other increase in owner's equity and is calculated before any expenses are subtracted. Net income can be calculated by subtracting expenses from revenue.

➢Premises（营业场所）

Premises are land and buildings together considered as a property. In this sense, the word is always used in the plural, but singular in construction. Not that a single house or a single other piece of property is "premises", not a "premise", although the word "premises" is plural in form as in "The equipment is located on the customer's premises" and never "The equipment is located on the customer's premise".

➢Trade fair（商品交易会）

An exhibition at which companies in a specific industry can show or demonstrate their products.

➢Understaffing（人员不足）

Not having enough workers, or fewer workers than usual.

➢Wholesale（批发）

To sell goods and services to those buying for resale (e. g. a shop) or for business use.

➢Outlet（经销店）

An outlet store is a retail store in which manufacturers sell their stock directly to the public through their own branded stores. The stores can be brick and mortar or online. Traditionally, a factory outlet was a store attached to a factory or warehouse often these stores are grouped together in outlet malls.

➢HR department（人力资源部）

The Human Resources department, working with people from other departments, is responsible for the people in the organization. This often includes:

- Hiring (including recruiting candidates, the interview process, negotiations, and signing contracts)
- Employee benefits
- Training and continued professional development
- Annual appraisals (in many companies)
- Promotions and raises
- Warnings and layoffs

The HR department works with the employees' managers for some of these tasks.

➢Marketing department（营销部）

The marketing department plays a vital role to the sales department. The main thrust is to make the product look and feel attractive enough to purchase. There are many things that the marketing department does. It creates and administers the advertising of a product...usually from conception to completion. In other words it develops the advertising campaign and works with the public relations department to place ads in various trade magazines and newspapers so that people and companies will see what you have. It develops the spec sheets that are used to promote interest at trade shows. It has responsibility for trade shows. Displaying the product, having literature ready, having the proper people available to talk about the product. It develops campaigns to promote the product to distributors and customers. It develops the branding...for instance the logo, the slogan, which will be used in advertising. It creates the kits or packaging that the product will be housed in. It is responsible for all press releases. To summarize, it creates the campaigns that make the product attractive to purchase, either by customers directly or by distributors who will sell the product for you.

➢Invoice（发票）

An invoice or bill is a commercial document issued by a seller to the buyer, indicating the products, quantities, and agreed prices for products or services the seller has provided the buyer. An invoice indicates the buyer must pay the seller, according to the payment terms. From the point of view of a seller, an invoice is a sales invoice. From the pint of view of a buyer, an invoice is a purchasing invoice.

➢Employee bonus schemes（员工奖金计划）

Bonus schemes and employee rewards strategies are established to fulfill a number of key business and HR objectives:

- To improve business performance (e. g. productivity, sales or profits).
- To focus employees' efforts on key objectives such as customer service, quality and on-time delivery.
- To increase employee motivation by establishing a clear link between pay and performance (at an individual or team level).
- To support stakeholder ideals by allowing employees to share in the success of the business.
- To encourage change within the organization.
- To create the desired workplace culture by, e. g. rewarding teamwork and good attendance.

➢Viral marketing（病毒式营销）

The viral marketing or viral advertising refer to marketing techniques that use preexisting social networks to produce increases in brand awareness or to achieve other marketing objectives (such as product sales) through self-replicating viral processes, analogous to the spread of pathological and computer viruses. It can be word-of-mouth delivered or enhanced by the network effects of the Internet.

Viral promotions may take the form of video clips, interactive Flash games, advergames, ebooks, brandable software, images, or even text messages. The basic form of viral marketing is not infinitely sustainable.

➢Staff training（员工培训）

When your staff have the right skills to do the best job, your productivity and competitiveness improves. Trained staff improve their contribution in the workplace, have more confidence in their abilities and more pride in their skills. This leads to a better quality of service for your customers. Train to Gain is designed to make it easier and more affordable for you to improve the skill levels of your staff. It's a fact, a well-trained workforce can have a measurable impact on performance and the bottom line.

➢Paid holiday（带薪假期）

Paid holidays are a normal part of a compensation and benefits package offered by employers to attract and retain employees. They are usually listed in an employment offer letter and appear in an employee handbook.

➢Level of customer satisfaction（顾客满意度）

Customer satisfaction is a measure of how products and services supplied by a company meet or surpass customer expectation. It is seen as a key performance indicator within business. In a competitive marketplace where businesses compete for customers, customer satisfaction is seen as a key differentiator and increasingly has become a key element of business strategy.

8. 英式英语和美式英语的区别

BEC 中级写作可以采用英式拼写或美式拼写，但考试时需要采用一种，必须前后一致。

➢英式美式拼写与词汇差异 Spelling & Vocabulary

– our/ – or

Many words end in – our in Britain, and in – or in America.

Here are some examples:

Britain	America
colour	color
favour	favor
neighbour	neighbor

– tre/ – ter

Words ending in – tre in Britain, end in – ter in America, for example:

Britain	America
centre	center
litre	liter
theatre	theater

Doubling of Letters:

In Britain, the "l" is doubled in an unstressed syllable:

Britain	America
travelling	traveling
marvellous	marvelous

Different spelling:

Britain	America
analyse	analyze
catalogue	catalog
cheque	check
defence	defence/defense
kerb	curb
plough	plow
pyjamas	pajamas
tyre (for a wheel)	tire

Different words:

Britain	America
handbag	purse/pocketbook
holiday	vacation
lorry	truck
motorway	freeway
nappy	diaper
pavement	sidewalk
tap	faucet

➤英式美式动词差异 Verbs

Verbs ending in – "ize" or " – ise"

In Britain, some verbs end in either – **ize** or – **ise**. Both are used.

In America, they always end in – **ize**.

examples: apolog**ise**/apolog**ize**

organ**ise**/organ**ize**

real**ise**/real**ize**

Regular-Irregular forms

Some verbs have alternative regular and irregular past tense and past participle forms, for example: **dream-dreamed or dreamt.** In Britain, the irregular form is more often used, whereas in American English, there is a preference for the regular form.

Here are some of those verbs:

dream dreamed/dreamt

learn learned/learnt

spell spelled/spelt

spoil spoiled/spoilt

and also:

dive-dived-dived (GB)

dive-dove-dived (US only)

➢英式美式代词差异 The Pronoun "one"

Americans do not often use "**one**" to mean "people in general", nor do they use "**one's**" or "**oneself**".

GB: One should look after one's health.

US: You should look after your health.

People should look after their health.

➢英式美式日期差异 Dates

There are differences in the way dates are said and written.

GB: 4th July – the fourth of July

US: July 4 – July four or July fourth

GB: 6/12/99 means the 6th of December 1999

US: 6/12/99 means the 12th of June 1999

➢英式美式数字差异 Numbers

The British use "**and**" between **hundred** and **the rest of the number**. The Americans leave it out.

GB：Two hundred **and** twenty.

US：Two hundred twenty.

主要参考文献

1. 何光明,《新国际商务英语写作》, 上海教育出版社, 2005 版。

2. 王战平,《新编剑桥商务英语中级精编》, 暨南大学出版社, 2007 版。

3. Guy Brook – Hart, Business Benchmark Upper-Intermediate, 牛津大学出版社(中国大陆销售), 2006 版。

4. 剑桥大学考试委员会外语考试部, 剑桥 BEC 真题集第 4 辑 (中级), 人民邮电出版社, 2009 版。

5. Russell Whitehead & Michael Black, 新编剑桥商务英语自测练习与解答(中级), 经济科学出版社, 2004 版。

6. 剑桥大学考试委员会外语考试部, 剑桥商务英语证书模拟试题册 (中级), 人民邮电出版社, 2004 版。

7. University of Cambridge ESOL Examinations, *Cambridge English Business Certificate Handbook for Teachers*, Cambridge University Press, 2008.

8. University of Cambridge ESOL Examinations, *Business English Certificate VANTAGE Examination Report*, Cambridge University Press, 2008.